MANAGE
YOUR TIME
& YOUR
LIFE

Other Titles of Interest from LearningExpress

Write & Speak Like a Professional in 20 Minutes a Day

MANAGE YOUR TIME & YOUR LIFE

MIRIAM SALPETER

NEW YORK

Published in the United States by LearningExpress, LLC, New York.

Cataloging-in-Publication Data is on file with the Library of Congress.

ISBN 978-1-61103-056-3

Printed in the United States of America

9 8 7 6 5 4 3 2 1

For more information on LearningExpress, other LearningExpress
products, or bulk sales, please write to us at:
    224 W. 29th Street
    3rd Floor
    New York, NY 10001

CONTENTS ▶

CONTENTS

CONTENTS

CONTENTS

About the Author

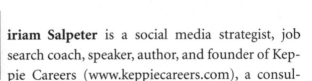

Miriam Salpeter is a social media strategist, job search coach, speaker, author, and founder of Keppie Careers (www.keppiecareers.com), a consultancy serving businesses and job seekers. Forbes named Miriam's blog a "best career resource" and CNN called her a "top 10 job tweeter you should be following." Top media outlets, including *The Wall Street Journal*, *The New York Times*, *Business Insider*, and others, recognize Miriam as an expert resource for job seekers and entrepreneurs.

Author of *Social Networking for Career Success* (in its second edition) and *Write & Speak Like a Professional in 20 Minutes a Day*, and co-author of *100 Conversations for Career Success* and *Social Networking for Business Success*, Miriam is well known as a go-to expert and consultant regarding job search and social media strategies.

In addition to coaching job seekers and small business owners, Miriam is an in-demand writer, speaker, and trainer for groups and organizations. She authors articles for company blogs and teaches job seekers and employees how to use social media. Miriam also runs "The Smart Business Owner's Social Media Help

Desk," an online program to teach business owners how to leverage social media marketing tools. She authors online bios and job search materials for clients at every level of their careers.

With a BA in Honors English from the University of Michigan, Miriam launched her career with a Wall Street firm. She left as a vice president to earn a master's degree from Columbia University with a focus on career guidance. Miriam headed the Career Action Center at the Rollins School of Public Health of Emory University before launching Keppie Careers. She has been empowering job seekers and small business owners since 2003.

Miriam lives in Atlanta with her husband, Mike, their three boys, two cats, and two rescue dogs. She invites you to connect with her on Twitter @Keppie_Careers and to touch base via her blog.

Acknowledgments

I n one book I remember fondly from my childhood, *The Phantom Tollbooth*, by Norton Juster, the Terrible Trivium teases Milo, the protagonist, by saying:

> *If you only do the easy and useless jobs, you'll never have to*
> *worry about the important ones which are so*
> *difficult. You just won't have the time. For there's always some-*
> *thing to do to keep you from what you really should be doing,*
> *and if it weren't for that dreadful magic staff, you'd never know*
> *how much time you were wasting.*

Don't we all have a "Terrible Trivium" in our lives—something tempting us away from the important things that should have our attention and time? I'm thankful for the opportunity to have tackled the many trivial (and not-so-trivial) forces in my life to write this book. Perhaps it's ironic, or maybe poetic justice, that the timing for this project brought so much of the advice here into focus for me!

This book is proof that we can all find the time to achieve our important goals. I always say that the best part about writing a book is finishing it. I'm thankful for the many people who inspired me when I wrote this book. A special shout-out to my friends who were encouraging and understanding, and consistently checked in to ask how I was coming along with my writing projects. I appreciate your support and confidence.

As with all of my books, my social media network played a role, providing a consistent stream of useful information (and, admittedly, distractions). Thank you to Sheryl Posnick, founder and president of Red Letter Content, for your editorial contributions and suggestions to ensure that this book is an invaluable resource for readers.

I couldn't run Keppie Careers and take on big projects such as this without the consistent support and partnership of my wonderful husband, Mike. I'm very lucky to be married to such a special person.

I dedicate this book to our three boys, with a wish that you each learn to spend time on what's most important—so you can identify the best ways to pursue and achieve your goals.

Introduction

Are you overwhelmed by life's details? Whether you're looking for a job, or you're fully ensconced in a career, do you feel like you're always running to catch up, and never completely in control of your day-to-day work and home life? This book is for you!

Manage Your Time & Your Life in 20 Minutes a Day provides suggestions and recommendations to help you make the most of every hour of the day. The result? You'll have more time for everything that matters to you, and you'll be able to successfully achieve your professional goals. No one has time to waste! That's why this book starts out by illustrating how to network effectively and how to choose the best jobs to apply for—to avoid the dreaded "resume black hole"—when employers ignore you. (After all, you never know when you'll want to look for a new opportunity.) If you already have your dream job, you can dive directly into the slew of best practices and ideas included in the majority of the book, which is dedicated to helping manage your time for professional success.

We cover the entire gamut: from how to incorporate healthy routines (such as what to eat and how to make time to exercise) to how to set and achieve your aspirational work goals. Whether you need help organizing your office, managing distractions at work, tracking your emails, or keeping a useful checklist and calendar, this book provides practical insights and information to help. If you haven't been tracking your wins at work, or you don't know what apps you should use to make the most of your time and avoid being distracted, we've got you covered!

Manage Your Time & Your Life in 20 Minutes a Day is an all-in-one efficiency guide, with suggestions to help you identify key action items and take the necessary steps to accomplish your short-term and long-term goals. Learn how to get a firm handle on your schedule to keep efficiently moving forward with your professional plans. Do you need help separating your "must do" from your "want to do" items? Could you use help to overcome procrastination and learn to become accountable for your plans? Would you appreciate advice about how to stop wasting time, effort, and energy? This book includes techniques and ideas to help you get organized and keep on track.

The result: You will be able to quickly review your progress, assess your strategies, and make positive changes. Are you ready to put the right combination of action items in place and just get things done? Let's get started!

MANAGE YOUR TIME & YOUR LIFE

I

HOW TO MANAGE A TIMELY JOB SEARCH STRATEGY

CHAPTER

Planning a Time-Effective Job Search

Looking for a job can absolutely be a full-time job in itself. The key to success (as well as your biggest challenge) is learning how to use your time well to help you land a new opportunity. If you don't take the time to come up with a solid plan, it can be very detrimental to your professional future. If you make errors, you'll never be able to regain your wasted time and efforts, and you'll set yourself back in your goals.

The information in this chapter will give you concrete goals to follow, so you can make the most of your precious job-search time. If you follow the advice here, you'll avoid feeling like you are spinning your wheels without making forward progress toward your goals.

Don't Take All Job Search Advice to Heart

Job seekers are magnets for well meaning, but ill-fitting, advice. Like moths to a flame, friends and family come out of the wood-work to explain what you should do if you want to land a job. Much of the time, these unsolicited advisors have stories about how someone they know did X, Y, or Z and found a job in a week. They want to critique your resume and your choice of interview outfits and second-guess your social media choices.

If you keep up-to-date on job search trends and read current information about how to market yourself for your target audience, ignore most of this well-intended advice. Don't waste time rewriting your resume based on each new suggestion or comment. Unless your advisors hire people for a living or work as job search coaches, it's likely their ideas are outdated (at best) or damaging (at worst). As long as you're conducting due diligence and keeping abreast of current trends, nod politely and move on.

Network Productively

Someone (perhaps one of those well meaning, but uninformed "advisors") may have suggested that you should tell everyone you meet you are looking for a job—from people online at the coffee shop talking about your field of choice to distant cousins in far-away states. Don't be surprised if that approach to professional networking fails. When you introduce yourself to people with the news you're looking for a new job and immediately ask if they can introduce you to someone at his or her place of employment or in your profession, that isn't networking. Networking isn't about asking for assistance or collecting names; it's about building relationships and helping others.

When you network, introduce yourself as the professional you are. Ask good questions and provide useful information and advice whenever possible. Avoid wearing a metaphorical "J" for job seeker on your forehead. People may respond politely, but it's unlikely they will provide useful resources for you. Ultimately, you'll waste a lot of networking efforts and your time using this technique.

Avoid expending a lot of time and effort at events where you meet people who never respond to your follow-up emails or who brush off your requests for in-person meetings. Instead, find new avenues for networking, including interest-oriented (not necessarily professional) groups: hiking clubs, book clubs, gardening clubs, wine-tasting societies, a local soccer league, or anything you feel passionately about where like-minded people will attend. In addition, turn to social media tools to leverage networks of people who are motivated to keep in touch. Unless you're attending groups with a reputation for shunning outsiders until they've attended a certain number of functions but somehow have a reputation for making up for it with networking gold once you've reached their designated milestone, do not waste your time networking with people who do not reciprocate.

THE IMPORTANCE OF MAKING CONNECTIONS

Dedicate most of your designated job search time to networking. CareerXRoads, an international consulting practice that surveys corporations about their recruiting and hiring practices, found that referrals (when a current employee suggests a candidate for consideration) are top sources of hire. Their report says, "A job seeker who is referred is conservatively three to four times more likely to be hired (some studies found that a job seeker who is referred is 14 times more likely to be hired) than someone who applies for a position without a referral." This is a persuasive statistic, which will hopefully convince you to prioritize networking when you plan your job search time.

Follow Up After Networking

You know you've wasted your time if you say you're going to be in touch, and never follow up. The best way to follow up is often via social media channels. Plan ahead before you set out to network with someone, to set up your follow-up steps. First, always remember to ask new contacts if you can invite them to connect via LinkedIn. Then, send the invitation directly from each person's LinkedIn page so you can personalize your invite and avoid sending LinkedIn's canned invitation. If you and your new contact both use other social networks, such as Twitter, reconnect using those channels, too. Don't move too quickly to become Facebook friends; save that for if you get to know the person better. On Twitter, include the person's username for that network in your message. For example:

> *@NewContact: I enjoyed speaking with you at _____ event last night. Will follow up re: suggestions we discussed.*

Take the Time to Digitally Demonstrate Your Expertise

Include time on your job search schedule to network via social media. It's never been easier to showcase your skills and background to a myriad of people. Use LinkedIn, Twitter, Facebook, and other relevant tools to prove you have the skills and background to do whatever is your desired job. These networks are especially helpful for people who want to transition to a new field. You can prove you're an expert in the new field, even if you don't have work experience in that area.

For example, if your job is to help orient new employees, you may post something such as:

> *What businesses can learn from onboarding practices of the @USArmy// I love #2: http://kell.gg/1m1Ub4j via @KelloggSchool*

Maybe you are transitioning from a corporate business and hope to work in a wellness industry. You may post updates to your social media feeds that suggest your interest in health topics:

> *No surprise. Walking everywhere helps you stay healthier, via @FastCompany: http://ow.ly/VVv2V*

> *Yoga is a healthy way to relieve stress. Here are tips for yoga you can do at your desk, via @HarvardBiz: http://ow.ly/VVB0J*

If you want to connect with an influencer in a field that interests you, social media can help. Write an update that includes the person's Twitter name. That way, he or she is likely to notice you. For example:

> *I agree with @Influencer. These are great success tips for new entrepreneurs: http://ow.ly/VCKRx*

Always update (or create, if you don't already have one) an optimized LinkedIn profile to supplement your most recent application materials. Studies show 94 percent of employers use LinkedIn as a repository of potential applicants. In addition, most employers will review your LinkedIn profile if they are considering your candidacy, even if you applied via a resume and cover letter. Target your profile for the type of positions you seek—be sure you include links to work products or presentations, if applicable, and ask for recommendations and endorsements on LinkedIn. You don't want your profile to be generic; it should support your candidacy. Refining your LinkedIn profile is time very well-spent. Do not fail to fill out this crucial profile, and always keep it up-to-date, even when you are not seeking a new job.

Preparation and research are key for every aspect of the job hunt, from identifying target companies and positions, to writing great marketing materials, to getting ready for interviews. If you schedule a meeting or attend a networking event without first taking time to make sure you've finished the research you need to do to make the most of the opportunity, you've wasted precious time.

The Biggest Job Search Time Wasters—and How to Avoid Them

Job seekers complain bitterly about applying for positions and never hearing back. There are ways to avoid this uncomfortable and annoying situation, but it takes some work on your part. Consider the following when you apply for jobs, and you'll save yourself a lot of aggravation.

Avoid the Internet Black Hole

It happens to everyone—you get online to do one thing, such as find new jobs to apply for or to search for new keywords to include in your resume, and the next thing you know you're checking Facebook, commenting on someone's new hairstyle or congratulating a friend on his or her engagement. Then, you make a quick diversion to check email (maybe an employer got back to you). Before you know it, you forgot what you were doing in the first place! Your biggest time wasters happen when you take unscheduled breaks from what you are doing and get distracted with something that is easier or more appealing. If this happens to you, try to be more disciplined about your job search efforts. If you're careful with your time, you'll be more likely to apply for appropriate jobs. Don't let yourself stop what you're doing to check email, and set a designated time to check social media sites and post your professional content. You'll get a lot more done in a lot less time.

If this sounds like a problem you face, put some mechanisms in place to avoid them. Plan ahead so you'll know what companies interest you—so you'll avoid being aimless online. Set a timer for at least 20 minutes and only conduct job-search business until it goes off. Review tips in Chapter 5 for apps that help you use your time well online.

Don't Apply for Jobs You Don't Want—Or Are Not Qualified to Do

Are you the job seeker who applies for every open position at a company? Do you think recruiters don't notice you've blanketed their systems, hoping they will find you a match? You can't possibly be truly qualified for—or want to work in—all of those positions. When you spend time applying for jobs this way, you're sending out red flags to hiring professionals at those companies and spinning your wheels in your job search. This is a big waste of time.

Just because you can apply for every job does not mean you should. Don't be like the kid who grabs a handful of candy just because it's there—be selective and apply for the jobs you're most qualified to do. When you apply for every job, recruiters and hiring managers will identify you as unfocused, and you aren't likely to land any interviews. Review the suggestions in Chapter 2 for advice about how to evaluate your skills and compare them to your target companies' needs.

Always Follow Application Instructions

Assume that when employers receive many responses, they immediately eliminate resumes from people who failed to follow instructions. Don't be one of those people. For example, if the employer requests a cover letter, you *must* include one—yes, no matter how annoying and time-consuming they are to write.

There's nothing worse than realizing you missed a key instruction relating to a job application after the fact. Slow down and take your time with each application you submit and you'll accurately apply for more appropriate jobs in the long run.

Follow Up with Employers

Designate time to follow up with employers in your job search schedule. Whether it's following up to find out the status of your application or writing a detailed thank you note, these are important "to do" items. You might think saying, "thank you" is so basic, and everyone must do it. You would be wrong! Many candidates fail to take this easy, courteous step. Within 24 hours, but ideally as soon as you return home after the interview, you should send thank you notes to the interviewer or interviewers. (Yes, you do need to write a personalized note to each person who spoke to you. Review the template in Chapter 3 to learn the type of information to include in a thank you note.)

Don't Harass Recruiters

Did you know that most recruiters are in business because companies expect them to source and help hire people so unique, they call them "purple squirrels?" In other words, recruiters want to find people who only exist in dreams! Unless you have extremely unique and special skills and work in a highly sought after field where it is difficult to source candidates, it's unlikely recruiters will be very interested in you. If recruiters do not pursue you and ask for follow-up information, it's not in your best interest to keep contacting them. Save yourself some time: touch base once or twice, and if they do not reciprocate your interest, move on and spend your valuable time elsewhere.

Don't Put All Your Hopes and Dreams in One Job

Never sacrifice all of your time, effort, and energy for one job. Diversify your efforts so you never count on one opportunity to come through. Unfortunately, even if your interview went well and it seemed like a perfect match, a lot of factors affect whether or not you win the job. Spread out your efforts and pay attention to a variety of positions. Keep researching new opportunities and spread out your networking so you won't rely on one or two jobs to come through.

Never Give Up or Act Bitter

No one wants to be around—or much less, hire—someone who acts bitter or gripes about his or her situation at every opportunity. Especially if you are spending a lot of time looking for a job, it's very tempting to lash out and blame other people for your situation. Even if you were laid off, don't fall into the trap of becoming a Negative Nellie or a Sad Sam. While you have a right to experience your frustrations, take them out at the gym, do not share them when you network or talk to contacts. Do not vent in public (or via social media), and do not point the finger at other people to explain your situation. People who seem to listen to you sympathetically when you vent are likely making mental notes not to introduce you to anyone they have in their networks. Take the high road and avoid burning bridges. You will save yourself time in the long run, and a positive attitude may help convince someone to introduce you to a great contact.

In Summary: Action Tips

Don't waste time when you're looking for a job. Follow these tips to help plan a timely, efficient job search strategy.

- Evaluate job search advice before you stop everything and change what you're doing. Don't blindly listen to everyone who has suggestions for you, especially if they haven't looked for a job or hired anyone in years.
- Pick networking events carefully and never introduce yourself first as a job seeker. Prepare to introduce yourself and learn about the people and organizations where you want to work.
- Spend time networking. Remember, studies show a job seeker who is referred is 14 times more likely to be hired than someone who applies for a position without a referral. Follow up after networking, or the people you meet will not remember you.
- Don't fall down the Internet black hole. Pay attention to how much time you spend online and have a goal in mind when you use the computer.
- Only apply for jobs you want and that you're qualified to do.
- Follow application instructions and follow up with employers after you apply. However, if a recruiter doesn't get back to you after a few contacts, he or she probably isn't interested. Save your time, effort, and energy and move on.
- Don't put all of your hopes and efforts into one job.
- Keep a positive attitude and don't let people think you are bitter or angry.

Time-Saving Tips to Create Winning Job Search Materials

I f you don't plan your time wisely, the job search can seem like a never-ending task. Employers admittedly control much of the process and hold all the cards when it comes to notifying (or not notifying) people when they fill positions. In spite of this, you as a job seeker can manipulate many job search factors to save time, effort, and energy—which, when combined with the tips from Chapter 1, will eventually lead to your desired result. Read on to learn the best way to create materials that will help you find jobs that interest you and get advice to help you evaluate and revise your job search materials.

Identify Companies That Interest You

Save time by looking for a *company* instead of a job. When you overfocus on jobs and spend too many hours reviewing job boards or perusing posted listings, you may miss chances to learn about opportunities you may find via networking and to apply for unlisted positions that will never appear on job boards. Include both small and large companies in your research. If you're planning to stay in your current geographical area, focus on local companies; if you are willing to relocate, cast a wide net. Tap into business directories or your local business newspaper to identify companies to research. Google to find lists of best companies and search industry publications for organizations you may not have considered.

Focus on Your Skills

Identify the best skills you have to offer and don't waste time applying for jobs with employers who are not interested in your core skills. Delve into who you are as a person, not just who you are as an employee, and make sure not to ignore your soft skills or emotional intelligence. For example, are you an exceptional communicator? Do you have a knack for leading teams? Maybe you're a great negotiator? Purposefully select your best skills and identify fields or jobs where you can use them.

Exercise: Take time to identify and write down the answers to these questions. This information will help you plan your job search.

Honestly ask yourself and answer the following questions.

1. **What do supervisors tend to praise about my work?**

   _____

   _____

   _____

   _____

2. **What skills do I enjoy using, and use well?**

   _____

   _____

   _____

   _____

3. **Who am I as a person?**

   _____

   _____

   _____

   _____

   _____

4. **What activities at work make me happiest and most confident?**

   _____

   _____

   _____

   _____

   _____

5. **What do I offer that helps me stand out from a crowd of applicants?**

_____

_____

_____

_____

_____

6. **Which accomplishments am I proud to share with target employers?**

_____

_____

_____

_____

_____

7. **What do I enjoy outside of work?**

_____

_____

_____

_____

_____

If you don't know the answers to any of these questions, allot the time necessary to explore and answer them. Connect the dots between what you want to do and what you have done well in the past.

If you're considering a career shift or change, it's worth your time to hone in on what you know about yourself, beyond what you normally consider your professional skills. Self-evaluate regularly. Explore your skills—both in and out of work—and leverage the information you find to help decide what jobs are best for you.

Once you know what you have to offer, carefully review job descriptions and read companies' online profiles on all the big social networks. For example, review their websites, LinkedIn, and company Facebook profiles and check YouTube and Twitter for details to help you identify how to create materials that will put you ahead of the crowd. When you know what the hiring managers want, you'll save yourself a lot of time by applying for the jobs you're qualified to do.

If a company features a particular skill set in their company profile, and you offer a strong match for that skill, highlight the match in your materials. For example, if the phrase "team player" appears on everything the company publishes online, that's a clue for you to describe what a great team player you are at work! Another item some job seekers fail to capitalize on is if the company has a specific mission or vision that matches what's important to you. For example, if the company posts YouTube videos showing team members volunteering at schools or building homes for Habitat for Humanity, and you are an active volunteer, you'll want to indicate your interest in serving the community in your materials.

Target Your Materials

Just as it's a bad idea to apply for every job at one organization, it's a waste of time to send the exact same resume to apply for 100 different jobs in various companies. Instead of blanketing your resume, target jobs you really want and that you're actually qualified to do. Select jobs based on how good of a fit they are for your skills and qualifications. Scan resumes for skills and keywords that resonate with you, and that you can adequately document in your materials.

Exercise: Find Your Keywords

Choose several job descriptions that interest you. Copy and paste the information into a file and highlight all of the parts of the descriptions that apply to you. Ideally, you will highlight all (or most) parts of the materials. Re-review the highlighted details and underline all of the words that seem to come up more than once. Those are most likely to be the keywords you should include in your resume. Make a list here of the most important keywords:

_____

_____

_____

_____

_____

_____

_____

Once you identify the overlap between what employers want and what you offer, create bullet points for your resume to explain how and why you are a good fit.

For example, if the position description requires you to be able to maintain accurate records, function in a fast-paced office, and provide reports, one of your bullet points may say:

> *Maintained confidential records for all physicians in fast-paced, busy office. Accurately reported numbers of patients and tallied insurance figures at end of each business day, resulting in more efficient, effective office.*

Write bullet points that feature keywords and skills from the job descriptions you selected and highlighted.

_____

_____

_____

_____

_____

_____

_____

_____

_____

_____

AVOID APPLICATION MISTAKES

Once you've identified employers, honed in on your skills, targeted your materials with keywords, used social media, and updated your documents, you're ready to apply for jobs. Spend the necessary time to make sure you address your materials to the right employer and don't mistakenly send a resume or cover letter intended for one employer to a different employer. Proofread your materials closely before you apply. Especially if you're a perfect fit for the job, you don't want to ruin your chances to win an interview with hastily written materials that have typos.

Evaluate Your Resume

While employers review online profiles and information you post on social media, your resume is still one of the most important parts of your job search materials—it's the one item 99% of postings will ask you to provide. If you have a sub-par resume, you likely won't get a chance to even have an interview—making your entire application process for every company you reach out to a waste of your time. Use these tips to help create a document that makes companies take notice.

Don't Include Too Much in Your Resume

One common waste of time and space is creating a resume that can double as an autobiography. Depending on your level of experience, your resume should probably be one or two pages long. (One rule of thumb is one page for 10 years of experience or less and two pages for more than 10 years of experience.) In some cases, a longer resume may be appropriate, but don't be compelled to include irrelevant details (such as computer programs no one uses anymore) or information that has nothing to do with your current goal. Pare down the details so they are concise and relevant for your current target employer.

It's also a waste of time to add details no one expects to see in your resume. For example:

- Leave off the objective, as it's a relic from the old days when resumes were more about what job seekers wanted. Today, employers want to know what you can do for *them*; they aren't interested in your wish list.
- Never include the line, "References available upon request." Everyone assumes you'll provide references. In addition, with all of the information available online, most employers don't even need references from you to help them contact someone to discuss your abilities; they can easily find people to contact on their own.

Modernize Your Resume

There's nothing worse than realizing (too late) that you've been applying for positions without the requisite keywords that will get it noticed, and that your resume looks like it's from the 1990s. (For example, you list an objective, include "references upon request," and detail unnecessary, dated skills.) Review job descriptions and ask yourself, "Does my resume make a clear connection between what the employer wants and what I offer?" Be sure the link between your skills and the employer's needs is obvious; do not expect anyone to give you the benefit of the doubt or to read between the lines on your resume. When you do apply online for jobs, an applicant tracking system will scan and evaluate your materials; be very clear and specific about your skills if you want to land interviews.

Check your resume for these overly self-centered red flags that will prevent employers from pursuing your candidacy.

An Objective

Does your resume include a line or two at the top such as: "Seeking a position with a growing company where I will feel fulfilled and get experience necessary to achieve my goals"? While most objectives are not quite so self-centered, the nature of the objective is that it focuses on the job seeker and not the employer. In other words, it's all about you and what *you* want. The employer does not care about your needs, so any language focused on you is a waste of space on your resume. In addition, the objective is a dated vestige of resume days gone by; avoid it in favor of a "headline" and quick bullet points that clearly connect with the employer's needs.

I, Me, or My

While some resumes do include first-person language, in general, resumes should be written in the first-person-implied perspective. For example, "Managed 20 employees" instead of "I managed 20 employees." If your resume is peppered throughout with self-referential language, it will probably strike the reader as a bit "me-centric."

Oversharing

It's very nice that your family is the most important aspect of your life, but the resume isn't the place to discuss it. Refrain from including too much personal information that does not relate to the job's requirements. When you do spend too much space talking about yourself, it indicates you are preoccupied with what you want or need instead of what the employer wants from you. In the United States, resumes should never include personal information, such as age, marital status, or religious affiliation.

Seeking Experience

If you were hiring, would you choose someone who hopes to gain experience by doing the job or select a candidate who already has the needed skills? It's rare for an employer to hire someone who does not already have the background and skills necessary to do the job. If you are looking for experience, that is fine, but keep it to yourself and focus on the skills you do have to help qualify you for the job.

Unnecessary Details

You don't need to list every job you've ever held for the past 25 years on your resume. Generally, it's appropriate to include the last 10 or 15 years of experience, but focus on the most relevant experience. Especially if you're transitioning to a new field, feature the experience in past jobs that's more important and interesting to your new target employer. Don't waste time listing things you've done that have nothing to do with your goals.

Exercise: How many of these "don't do this" list items are on your resume? How do you plan to change these to ensure you have a more modern, useful marketing document?

_____

_____

_____

_____

_____

_____

_____

_____

_____

_____

_____

_____

_____

JOBSCAN.CO

An online tool to help you evaluate if you're a good match for a job is called JobScan.co (https://www.jobscan.co). Once you update your resume for keywords and fit, paste the job description and your resume text to see your results.

In Summary: Action Tips

Save time by using best practices to create your materials and to choose the best jobs for you. These tips will help ensure you focus your efforts in the right direction.

- Narrow your search by company instead of focusing only on job boards.
- Identify your best skills as they relate to the jobs that interest you. Conduct some self-discovery and figure out who you are as a person before you narrow your target organizations.
- Once you focus, target your materials using keywords to appeal to employers.
- Evaluate your resume to be sure it is modern and doesn't include irrelevant or self-centered details.

Preparing for Job Interviews

Every part of your job search preparation is valuable and important, but it's crucial for you to plan and prepare for interviews. Employers dismiss candidates who come to interviews unprepared; some hiring managers even consider it a personal affront to interview candidates who did not plan ahead to be able to answer typical questions, such as why they are the most qualified candidate and how the company is a good fit for them. Don't be the unprepared candidate. Use these steps to prepare for interviews, and you'll be on your way to job search success.

Researching Is Time Well-Spent

It's worth your time to research companies that interest you. If you don't, you'll never know what smart things you should say during the interview to impress hiring managers with your insights. Luckily, there are a lot of places to research both companies and individuals, and you can find most of the information you absolutely need from the comfort of your own home via your computer or mobile device.

Use the Organization's Website and Social Media Properties

The first place to look is the most obvious. The company's website and social media streams (LinkedIn, Twitter, Facebook, Instagram, Pinterest, and any other outlets) will showcase what the company values. However, don't just take the information at face value. Do they post about their people, or only feature the organization? Do they volunteer in the community? Are they a "work hard, play hard" organization? You'll probably be able to learn a lot just from reading what they publish. Follow their social media accounts if they post there and keep up with what they're doing and what they share.

On LinkedIn, when you visit a company's page you will be able to tell who in your network works for the organization or connects you to someone who does. Review profiles of people who work at companies that interest you. Learn about their backgrounds and skills and match your accomplishments when possible. Does everyone at a company have a history of previously working in a particular company? Perhaps that's a clue for you to start by trying to network your way into that organization as a stepping stone.

Review Glassdoor.com

This site collects information about and reviews of companies, including interview topics and questions. If there's a review about an interview for a position similar to your target job, you can probably focus your preparation time by following advice in the review. However, be aware that your interviewer may take a different approach, so always factor in enough time in your schedule to take the basic steps listed here to prepare.

BUILD YOUR RESEARCH TOOLBOX

While basic Internet and social media research will yield a lot of information, you may want to dig a little deeper to find details average applicants would never know. Tap into tools such as Zoominfo.com, OneSource, and LexisNexis. You may also try investigating Company Insight Center from *BusinessWeek*.

In addition, check out websites such as Hoovers, OneSource, and the EDGAR database for information about companies. While some of these are paid resources, your library may offer free access to patrons. Save time by sourcing information from a reference specialist. Ask your local librarian for other ideas of ways to research companies.

Leverage In-Person Networking

While it's great to research online, in-person networking can provide a fast track to help you learn a lot about organizations. Find networking groups in your area. Meetup.com is one resource to find groups in a variety of interest areas and Roundtown.com is another. Spend time on each of these sites to discover events to visit, to expand your network and to help you research various organizations.

Exercise: How to Efficiently Find People Who Can Help You Land a Job

Save time by planning your networking. Identify the information you want to know and who might be able to provide it. Start by listing five people (or job titles of people) you would like to meet. Include company names and any other details you already know. For example: Retail Buyer, Macy's, Jana Smith might know someone. List as much information as you can here to get started:

_____

_____

_____

_____

_____

_____

Once you identify people you want to meet, before your meeting, write down what you hope to learn from them. If you could find out any information about the organization, what would it be? Write down some questions specific to your needs:

_____

_____

_____

_____

_____

_____

At these meetings, you want to offer useful, helpful information and resources. What information do you think you can provide the people you meet? What part of your background would be most useful to inspire the people you want to meet to suggest others for you to meet? Consider your resume: What successes make you most proud? What problems have you been helpful in solving? What are your best skills? Write them down here:

_____

_____

_____

_____

_____

_____

Flaunt Your Research

During interviews, make it clear that you're prepared and have done research. Create opportunities during interviews to incorporate information you identified when you delved into the company's background.

For example, when the employer asks why you are interested in the job, you can begin your response, "I conducted a lot of research before I decided where to apply for jobs." Go on to explain exactly what you found, and don't hesitate to mention the resources you used. You don't need to feature every resource you touched when learning about the company, but it's a good idea to make it clear that you didn't just show up for the interview. One answer may sound something like this: "In my research, I spent a lot of time learning about your company by reading the streams of information available via social media. I was impressed by how involved and enthusiastic so many of the employees were when talking about their work and the difference they make for their clients. I also used Hoovers to learn about the company's competitors. Based on what I learned, I believe my skills would be a good fit here."

Using this simple technique, you'll make the most of the time you spent studying the organization and appear even more well qualified for the job because you went above and beyond the basic requirement of showing up for the interview.

Know Your Own Skills Before You Go In

Be very familiar with your own materials. You never know when someone will inquire about something you wrote and did not anticipate discussing. You don't want to be caught off guard during the interview. Evaluate your resume line-by-line and ask yourself, "What example would I give if someone asked me about this?" When you have an answer to each potential question about your skills and accomplishments, you'll be ready for interviews.

Exercise: How to Be Sure You Really Know What You Offer

Review your resume. Write down at least one example to discuss in an interview for each bullet point you list. For example, if you included "Organized files and created new system to find documentation, resulting in time and money saved," your example might be in the form of a story about how an executive wanted some old information from the archives and, because of your new system, you were able to deliver them in less than two hours when the average time might have been days or a week.

Use this space to create a checklist of information and stories based on your most important accomplishments from your resume.

What Questions Should You Prepare to Answer?

When you prepare to interview, it's tempting to believe the only way to win the job is to spend days or weeks memorizing answers for 500 possible interview questions. It's overwhelming, and luckily, it's not true. It is a good idea to research the organization, consider potential questions the interviewer may ask, and think about how you will respond, but it's a waste of time to try to memorize answers to hundreds of random questions you may never be asked.

Instead, the best and most important question you should spend time preparing is the one question every interviewer will ask (in some form): "Why should I hire you?" It is the underlying question behind every other interview question, It may take many forms, for example, "What do you potentially offer this organization?" or "Why are you the most qualified candidate?" Interviewers want to know they won't be making a mistake by hiring you.

Consider these four keys to addressing this underlying interview question:

- **Identify the connections between what the company needs and what you offer.** The job description is the best way to figure out what the organization wants. Study it, highlight it, and focus your attention on explaining why you are the person best suited to solve the organization's problems. Read everything you can about the company. Consider interview preparation to be a research project. Find out everything you can and put it to use. The more you know, the better you will be able to address the underlying question, "Why should we hire you?"
- **Prepare to discuss your past accomplishments specifically, as they relate to the organization's current needs.** "Past performance is not indicative of future results" is a common

disclaimer investment companies tell their customers. This doesn't apply when it comes to a job search; employers heavily weigh past performance when they evaluate you. Be prepared to point out specific instances describing when you've handled the kind of problems and challenges facing the person who will fill this role. If you worked as part of a team, make sure to specify your contributions. Don't be generic in your description. Avoid saying "we" or "the team" when you're specifying your contributions. Be clear about your roles in past successes so the employer understands exactly how you can use your skills if you join his or her organization.

- **Articulate your ideas.** Don't waste all of the research and information you've uncovered. Once you understand the problems facing the organization and the role you wish to fill, be prepared to talk about how you can tap your past experience to solve those problems. Employers do not spend the money to fill roles unless they have problems to solve. Do yourself and the interviewer a favor and make it clear how you might suggest addressing the issues. You'll be ahead of the majority of your competitors.

- **Incorporate your soft skills, such as positive attitude, communication skills, time management, and critical thinking, into your answers.** Otherwise known as emotional intelligence, soft skills may be the difference between an employee who can do the job and one who does it well. Whether they admit it or not, employers want to hire candidates who are likable and easy to get along with. A study from Millennial Branding showed soft skills topped the list of must-have skills that employers want, with 98 percent of employers saying communication skills are essential and 92 percent naming coordination skills.

What Questions Should You Prepare to Ask an Employer?

One of the biggest pet peeves hiring managers express is, "Interviewees do not come prepared for interviews." Employers complain when candidates haven't done research about the organization and when they cannot express why they are good fits for the jobs. On the other hand, when an interviewee asks a targeted, pointed question that gets to the root of what the hiring manager seeks, it speaks worlds for that candidate's ability to deliver.

Good Questions for Employers

- What is expected of the new hire? What is the #1 priority for the person hired for this job?
- What are the most important skills needed for someone to be successful here?
- What are the biggest challenges facing the organization, unit, or team?
- What are the most exciting opportunities coming up that will affect this position?
- Can I meet the people who would be on the team I would potentially join? (Don't assume the employer introduced you to the people you will see everyday at work.)
- What is it like to work here?

Questions That Are a Waste of Time

1. **Do not ask anything you can easily find online.** It makes you look like you're unprepared and just grasping for a question to ask. It's almost better to ask nothing than to ask something such as, "What are your most popular products?"
2. **Avoid any question that suggests you would want or need special favors.** This starts when you schedule your interview. If you start asking for special favors from the get-go, it's a red flag for employers. At the interview, don't

ask about working from home or flexibility. Since schedules are usually pretty standard (either set hours or all hours,) it's probably not helpful to ask about them in an interview.

3. **Avoid asking questions that seem self-serving.** For example, don't ask about benefits, vacation, or raises. That's something to address once they offer the job. Table questions about salary until it is time to negotiate.

4. **Anything that makes it appear you want this job to be a stepping stone to something else.** If you ask, "When could I apply for a promotion?" you're giving a clear message that you're already moving on from this job they are focused on filling. Most employers do not want to hire someone who has his or her eyes on the next thing. Keep your aspirations to yourself for the time being.

Plan for the
Day of the Interview

If you live in Atlanta and get a call to interview for a job in Tampa later in the week, but no one mentions anything about travel arrangements, it might be logical to assume it's a telephone or video interview. However, you should never assume anything regarding the details of your interviews. Always communicate about the specifics of the interview. For example, if you have an invitation to interview for a job in another city, you might respond:

> *I'm very interested in the XYZ position in Tampa, and I appreciate the opportunity to discuss my qualifications with the hiring manager. I am located in Atlanta. Will this be a telephone or video interview? If we will be meeting in person, is there a budget to cover my travel expenses, or will I be responsible for those costs?*

Asking questions demonstrates you are detail oriented, which is an important quality for almost every job. When you learn all the details you need to know, it makes it easier for you to plan ahead and arrange your time properly.

Identify Key Details

You do not want to flail around the morning of the interview finding out details you should have secured ahead of time. Know the answers to the following questions:

- What time is the interview?
- Where is the interview?
- What do you need to know about parking and other access issues?
- If it is a phone appointment, is the interviewer calling you or is it up to you to place the call?
- What phone numbers will everyone use?
- Who will be interviewing you? (Make sure to get the correct spellings of their names and also their contact information, so you can easily follow up with thank you notes.)

When the interview is remote it's very easy to muck up the specifics, but if you are waiting for a call and the interviewer expected you to initiate the conversation, you'll lose an opportunity. It's wise to send an email to confirm all the specifics so everyone is on the same page.

Make a Trial Commute to the Interview Location

The most important part of an interview is showing up, so don't forget to include a trial commute to get to the interview location. Allow yourself extra time in case there are any emergencies along the way. When you're on time and relaxed, it will be easier for you to communicate your skills and accomplishments to the interviewer.

Plan What to Wear

Is there anything more stressful than getting ready the morning of your interview and not being able to find your dress shoes, or learning your interview suit has a moth hole right in the front? You can divert these and other potential disasters by planning ahead. Ideally, you'll check all of these details before you even have an interview schedule. Is your interview outfit ready? Does it need dry cleaning? Are your shoes unscuffed and accessible? You may be called to interview at the last minute, so prepare to be ready to interview, even if you don't have much notice.

Set Everything Up in Advance

Collect everything else you may need for the interview. For example:

- A professional portfolio and/or briefcase
- Several copies of your resume
- A list of references
- Work products you plan to share at the interview
- A pad and pen
- A list of questions to ask
- Notes to remind you why you're a good fit for the job, to review while you're in your car or between meetings
- Your calendar, in case they want to schedule another meeting
- Business cards

If you have everything ready to go, you'll reduce your stress level and save time the morning of your appointment.

Interview Follow-Up

After the interview, send out thank you notes to everyone you met as soon as possible. Ideally, your notes will be done within 24 hours. Save effort by following a template such as the one below, but personalize every note and don't mass produce them—even if you met a lot of people.

Exercise: Thank You Note Template

Fill in the information immediately after your meetings and your thank you notes will practically write themselves:

Say "thank you," mention the name of the position, and list something specific about the meeting (such as, "I'm glad we were able to meet before you left for vacation" or "I appreciate you taking the time to answer all of my questions").

_____

What key points were discussed? Include the most important details or topics the employer focused on in the interview.

_____

_____

_____

Make a strong connection between your skills and the job. List several specifics that make you a good fit for the position.

_____

_____

_____

Reiterate your appreciation, indicate you hope the employer agrees you are a good fit, and note plans to keep in touch.

_____

_____

_____

_____

In Summary: Action Tips

If you're not ready for interviews, you'll waste all of your other preparation time. Use these tips and you'll be ready to explain why you're the best candidate for the job.

- Research organizations that interest you via their websites, social media properties, in-person conversations, and networking.
- Understand and be able to articulate your own skills.
- Showcase your research during the interview by being prepared to answer the questions employers are most likely to ask.
- Note the connections between your skills and what the company needs and prepare to feature them when you discuss your skills and accomplishments. Don't forget about your soft skills, such as your ability to communicate and work on teams.
- Prepare questions for the employer that reflect your research and demonstrate you're a good fit. Don't waste time asking things you can easily find out on your own.
- Plan for the interview in advance. You may not have much lead time when you're invited to an interview.
- Make sure you know all of the interview details, including location, date, and time. If the interview is in person, make a trial commute if possible.
- Plan what you'll wear, and collect all of the materials you'll need before the interview. Don't wait for the last minute.
- Follow up after the interview with targeted thank you notes.

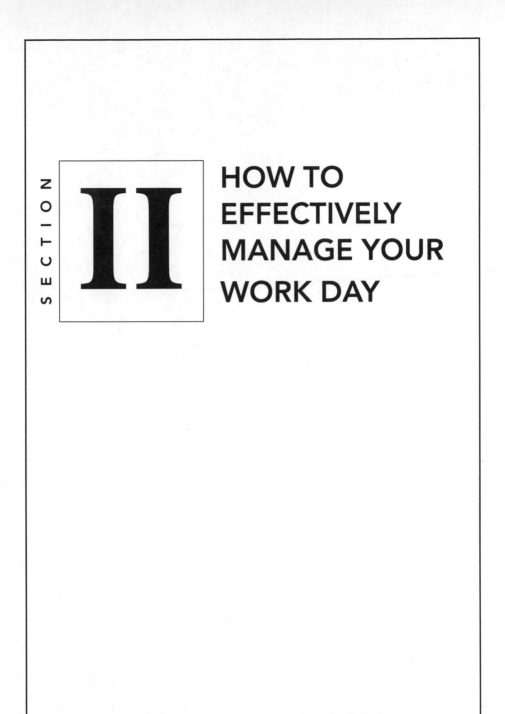

SECTION

II

HOW TO EFFECTIVELY MANAGE YOUR WORK DAY

CHAPTER

4

Preparing for Work the Night Before

You did everything right and landed the job! At this point, your planning and preparation should begin in earnest so you'll be able to manage and balance your time and your life in the wake of your new job. Of course, everyone's plans will vary, depending on how complicated (or not) their lives may be. If it's just you, you'll have a lot less to prepare. If many people count on you for daily activities, you will have more to juggle. With the right planning and list making, you'll be able to get everything done in a timely, efficient way.

In a word: plan! Preparation prevents problems (at least most of the time). When you plan ahead, you are bound to save time later. In addition, when you get into the habit of planning ahead (not just for the first day of work), it will become second nature, and you'll be more likely to maintain a rhythm that supports a strong balance between work and home. Don't let any item elude you when you prepare the night before—that way, you don't face any surprises when you wake up the next day. Everything will be all set!

Plan Out Your Transportation

Decide what time you need to leave your home in the morning in order to arrive at work at least five minutes before you have to be there. If you leave everything to chance and arrive late to work regularly, your co-workers will notice, and they will not appreciate it. Many people believe tardiness is rude (at best) and irresponsible (at worst). Even if no one ever says anything about your late arrival times, assume your colleagues will notice, and it may hurt your chances to succeed in the organization in the long run.

Add in an appropriate buffer for unexpected circumstances, such as an accident on the highway that delays traffic or an incident that slows down the public transportation you rely on to get to work. Ideally, you've done a test run to determine your commute's typical length before your first day. After you've tried out your commute for a while, you will be more familiar with obstacles that can pop up and make you late. Pay attention and adjust accordingly.

If you're driving, make sure your car has gas the evening *before*, so you don't need to make an unexpected stop to refuel on the way to work. If you take public transportation, ensure you are prepared to pay your fare so you aren't wasting time stuck in line.

You may want to also set up an app to help you navigate any unexpected traffic and to gauge the best route in the morning. Use your usual favorite, or try one of these suggestions:

- **Beat the Traffic:** Identifies delays along your route and can save routes to review later.
- **Waze:** A large community-based traffic and navigation app. Drivers share real-time traffic information.
- **InRix:** Updated via billions of data points in order to provide real-time traffic advice.

Select Your Clothing

Choose everything you plan to wear before you go to bed. Select all accessories—belt, shoes, jewelry—so you won't be hurried in the morning trying to find something you need to complete your outfit. Take care of all the details the night before: shine your shoes, iron your shirt or blouse, and make sure everything looks professional and appropriate. If you haven't tried on your outfit in a while, make sure to do so at this point. You should select something that makes you feel confident and comfortable. The key is not to be scrambling in the mornings to: a) make the decisions what to wear, b) see if it fits, and c) select and find all the items you need before leaving the house.

Prep for Small Talk

Have you kept up with the news and popular culture? Are you prepared for water cooler conversation with your colleagues? If not, perhaps it's time for a quick review of what people are discussing. One way to catch up on the news of the day is to review your Facebook feed for trending topics. It typically provides a clear view of topics that have people's attention. If you log into Twitter, you'll see trending topics as well. These topics may include anything from the latest celebrity scandal to news of the day and information about sports. Take a quick look at local and national news, too. If you review these items, you are unlikely to be caught offguard by most of the small talk you'll encounter at work.

Ready Your Personal Items

Charge your phone, select your purse or briefcase, and place all the necessary items inside, including your wallet, any IDs you'll need, mints, tissues, money (it's a good idea to have cash), a brush or comb, and other personal care items you may need.

All paperwork you'll need to take to work should be sorted, ready to go, and inside or next to your bag or briefcase. The last thing you want to do in the morning is run around searching for something necessary to be able to park in the lot or get in the door at work. Gather any mail or packages you need to send out, as well. Also, make sure you have phone numbers of people to call in case you have any unexpected problems and need to reach someone in your office.

Make a Plan for Your Family

Don't forget to make a plan for your family if you're responsible for other people. If you have children, is their plan set for the next day? Are their shoes at the door and ready to wear? Do they have all necessary clothing, lunches, and backpacks with completed homework and projects ready to go? If they're young, are diaper bags packed and ready? Do you have the necessary bottles or sippy cups, food, snacks, diapers, and changes of clothing? If it's up to you to help anyone else leave the house in the morning, include all of their items on your to-do list. You don't want anything holding you up!

Figure Out Your Food Situation

Health.com suggests you avoid foods high in fat, protein, or caffeine if you want a good night's sleep. Instead, they suggest you choose food and drink more favorable to helping you rest. Consider the following examples:

- Cherries—This fruit includes melatonin, which can be a sleep aid.
- Milk or turkey—These both contain tryptophan, which makes you sleepy.
- Complex carbohydrates—Cereal is a great choice, as are bananas.
- Magnesium and potassium—Bananas or sweet potatoes may help you drift into a good night's sleep.

A perfect evening snack may be a bowl of non-sugary cereal, such as shredded wheat with milk and a banana.

Plan for your meals and lunch for the next day, too. It's a great idea to shop and plan for meals for the whole week, so you're never coming home after a long day, only to realize you have no more supplies to make your lunch the next day! If you like to cook, consider making something you can partition out to eat for the next few days, such as a casserole or chili. Purchase easy-to-grab items in bulk for snacks or to supplement your meals, such as pre-packaged crackers or granola bars. Fruit is a healthy choice, portable, and easy to buy in advance. Stock up on the necessities, and you'll save time every night.

Sleep Smartly

Once you calculate how much time it will take to get to work and when you need to leave the house, factor in how much time you need to get ready in the morning. Think of ways to buy yourself some extra time in the morning. For example, would it help if you shower the night before? If you did a good job preparing everything in advance, hopefully you can expect a smooth morning. You may also want to build in a bit of extra time in case something unexpected comes up in the morning. Set your alarm for the designated time—with time to snooze if you know you're in the habit!

Get Enough Sleep

Practice good sleep habits. Give yourself every opportunity to sleep well by following a few guidelines:

- Avoid caffeine, nicotine, alcohol, or other foods and drinks that may keep you awake. Don't go to bed when you're hungry or overly full and limit how much you drink before sleeping.
- Experts advise that you avoid screen time right before bed and to avoid bright lights, including television. Also avoid watching shows you may find upsetting right before you go to sleep.
- If you have a good sleep routine or ritual, follow it. It's not ideal to start something brand new the night before you begin your job. If you already wind down with yoga, a warm shower, by listening to soothing music, or by reading a good book, keep those steps in your routine.
- Move your phone away from your bed so notifications in the middle of the night don't wake you up.

In Summary: Action Tips

Use the examples in this chapter to help construct a complete list of what you need to do to be prepared the night before you go to work. Review the categories for planning transportation, clothing, workplace conversation, paperwork, and personal items. Make a plan for the family. Prepare for food needs, plan when to wake up, and get enough sleep. Consider including items such as "shop for a cereal with complex carbohydrates" and "get gas for the car." Envision the night before you go to work, step-by-step, and add details specific to you and your situation. For example, if you need to secure childcare, include information about whom you will call. The more information you put on your list, the less stressed you are likely to be the night before you need to go to work.

Exercise: Make Your List

_____

_____

_____

_____

_____

_____

_____

_____

_____

Transportation

Include items you need to have, what you need to do, and what information you need to know.

_____

_____

_____

_____

_____

_____

_____

_____

_____

Clothing

Include what clothes you will wear and note if it needs to be cleaned or pressed, for example.

_____

_____

_____

_____

_____

_____

Paperwork

Consider all paperwork you need to bring to work: IDs, passports, other documentation, etc.

_____

_____

_____

_____

_____

Personal Items

Is there anything you don't want to forget?

_____

_____

_____

_____

Family Plan

Who relies on you in the morning? Note everything you need to do for those people.

_____

_____

_____

_____

_____

What to Eat

Do you need to shop for any best to eat items? What are some easy plans for lunch?

_____

_____

_____

_____

_____

Get Enough Sleep

Include what you will and will not do the night before to help you get some rest.

_____

_____

_____

_____

_____

Plan When to Wake Up the Night Before

Have you calculated how long you need in the morning? If you have any morning rituals, be sure to make time for them. In this section, add up the time it takes to do everything and calculate back the time to wake up.

ACTIVITY	TIME ALLOTTED
Time to wake up:	Time to leave home:

5 Making the Most of Your Time at Work

I f you followed the plan from Chapter 4, you will wake up with plenty of time to have a stress-free, unrushed morning. Don't underestimate how important it is to prepare in advance for career success; it's stressful to handle everything at the last minute. The best advice to keep in mind throughout your work day is to take care of your needs (such as lunch, comfortable clothing, and all of your work materials), and remain mindful throughout the day of what your boss and colleagues expect of you. When you plan in advance, your workday can run like clockwork and you'll accomplish everything you need to do.

Don't Skip Breakfast

You've heard that breakfast is the most important meal of the day. Even if you're strictly a "coffee for breakfast" aficionado, it can't hurt to make time for a real meal to start your day off right. Do you need some ideas for what to eat? Nutritionists recommend specific foods to help you concentrate—try something with high-fiber carbohydrates, healthy fat, and lean protein. For example, a whole grain piece of toast, avocado (healthy, unsaturated fats help brain cells), and an egg (a hard-boiled egg is portable if you eat on the go) would be good choices. Or, eat Greek yogurt with blueberries (great brain food) to help you start your day off well. Another good and easily portable choice: a whole wheat muffin with peanut butter and apple slices.

Exercise or Stretch

Do you have a daily exercise regimen? Even 20 minutes of physical activity daily can improve your health and give you a jumpstart for the day. Consider starting out with something low impact, such as yoga, to get you started. Or, if you can't imagine starting your day with exercise, consider another way to begin your day mindfully, such as meditation. If you don't believe you have time at home for exercise, think about ways to move more throughout your day. For example, take a walk during lunch, or ask a colleague if you can have a walking meeting. Even taking the stairs instead of the elevator a few times a day can make a small difference in your fitness routine. Take some time for yourself, even if its just for a few minutes at a time, and you may notice a difference in your mindset and in how you feel physically.

When to Arrive

There's an aphorism that goes "On time is late." In other words, you should always plan to get places early. Considering all of the factors outside of your control (traffic, transit, the late babysitter, the electricity went off, etc.), it makes sense to always plan to arrive at work early. If something unexpected comes up, hopefully, you'll still be on time.

Research suggests employers favor people who arrive early to work. It's not surprising. You know what they say, "The early bird gets the worm." There are many advantages to arriving early to work. If you're there before everyone else, you can take a few minutes to settle in and get ready for the day. An early arrival gives you time to review or set your priorities, organize your things, and get a cup of coffee. If anything surprising happened since you left, being early gives you a chance to catch up and mentally prepare for the new day. When you arrive early, people assume you are more attentive to detail than people who are on time or late, and it appears you are eager to work. These are highly sought after employee qualities.

How early should you arrive? Aim for 15 minutes at the least, but if you really want to make an impression, form a habit of coming in 30 or so minutes early every day. Even if no one else is there to assign you a gold star, you'll be able to use the time to settle in before a busy day. If you're really lucky, your boss or other influencers in the office will subscribe to the same theory of arriving at work early, and you'll curry favor with them.

Plan Your Work Day

You can use the same process to plan your day at work you used to plan your night before work. Take all stakeholder needs into account, including your own, your boss's, and your colleagues' when you plot out a targeted, efficient day.

Set Up Your Workspace
You may be familiar with the sarcastic quote, "A clean desk is the sign of a sick mind." Perhaps having an overly tidy workspace in a busy office may raise some eyebrows or cause people to wonder if

you do anything besides clean your desk! There is a happy medium, though. Whether or not you are a neat freak, your desk should be orderly enough that you can always find whatever you need. You'll know your workspace needs organizing when people ask you for items and it takes you 5 or 10 minutes of plowing through papers before you find what they need.

Consider the following suggestions to arrange and organize your desk and workspace.

Keep Everyday Supplies Handy

Do you struggle to find a pen? Can you never dig up a sticky note or a pad of paper? If you have to rummage around the office to find items you use everyday, you are wasting precious time you could otherwise use to get work done. Keep your desk drawer stocked with everything you need. If necessary, purchase items to help you keep everything organized or ask your office manager if you might be able to order one through the office. If you like to have items in plain sight, get a desk organizer with room for everything you use. Test yourself by keeping track of how often you need to stop what you're doing to find what you need. You'll know you're well organized when that number goes down to zero.

Limit the Personal Items You Keep

Too many photos or other personal items can be distracting and take up valuable real estate on your desk. If pictures and knick-knacks begin to crowd out actual work, you know it's time to pack up items to take home. Never keep old wrappers or soda cans on your desk. Garbage should go directly into the trash. If you eat at your workspace, clean up all the crumbs and associated mess. No one wants to see half-eaten sandwiches or empty microwave meal containers.

Clean Out Old Papers and Notes You Don't Need

Look through your drawers and remove everything you don't need. Keep organized trays with files accessible on your desk so you can easily segregate what you need to do (an action file) versus what you need to put away (a file folder). If you conduct any personal business from your desk (which is not a good idea, but realistically, most people do it), make sure your own paperwork doesn't get mixed up with your work files. Once you have a place for everything, it will be easier to keep organized. (Review Chapter 10 for more ideas about how to organize your workspace.)

Manage Distractions

Once your workspace is ready, try to manage distractions. Depending on your work environment, this may be challenging. If you have a door and an office, you may be able to shut your door during certain hours so you can focus on work. If you work in an open floor plan or in a cubicle, it may take a bit more creative planning to create a distraction-free environment.

Consider the following steps to improve your productivity at work.

Avoid Distractions in the First Place

How much of your lost productivity is your own fault? If you are distracted by your mobile device, put it away or turn it off so it doesn't tempt you. Consider that each time you respond to a quick text, you take time away from important projects at work. If you're too tuned into your personal life (for example, checking Facebook all day long or reviewing personal email), you'll lose important time you should have to get ahead with your work. If turning off your phone all day long makes you feel too disconnected, at least turn off notifications that aren't likely to be emergencies. Set your phone to only buzz if your child's school calls, for example. Or, designate break times during the day to check your messages, in case something is important. Do not allow your personal device to take you away from your work.

Stay Off the Internet

Do you spend a lot of time Googling topics or looking for information unrelated to work? That's a bad idea for many reasons, but most importantly, your IT department may be tracking your work online. If it turns out you spend hours each week (or each day) on non-work related tasks on your work computer, you may find yourself out of a job.

Limit Interruptions from Colleagues

Especially if you work in an open floor plan, it is very difficult to avoid interruptions. However, if you have too much engagement with colleagues, you may be losing valuable work hours every day. How can you plan to save time? Try to arrange your work space so you aren't facing the office. By turning your back (literally) on your colleagues, you may be able to capture some privacy and boost your productivity. Alternatively, you may want to ask if it's okay to wear noise-cancelling headphones to block out background noise if other conversations in the office are preventing you from getting your work done.

If possible, create times during your workday when you don't answer the phone or respond to emails or social media. If you have an idea that interrupts your flow, or you remember something you need to do, keep a notepad to write it down or add it to a list on an app you use so you don't forget.

Talk to colleagues and your supervisor and ask for uninterrupted time to get work done. Even consider putting up an "open office hours" or a "do not disturb" sign so people understand when you are available and when you need to focus. Another idea is to ask if you can work from home during certain days or hours if you believe it would be more productive without interrupting the normal workflow.

Beware of Oversocializing

If you're spending too much time in the break room or at the water cooler, take note and dial back your socializing. However, don't eliminate interactions with your colleagues entirely. Make a special effort to ask people to join you for lunch, or for a walk during your break. You don't want people to think you are antisocial, but you do want to curb the socializing to specific times of the day so you can leave on time and get all of your work done.

Avoid the Gossip Mill

While you're planning how to avoid distractions, remember to stay out of gossip sessions or other workplace drama that draws you in and takes up all of your time. Don't let your curiosity get the best of you. Stay away from spectacles and you'll be less likely to get distracted and fall behind. If you need proof of how much time you spend on productive versus non-productive activities during the day, try an app like Jiffy, RescueTime, or Chronos to time what you actually do during the day. Once you know how much time you waste, you may be motivated to make a change! Stay away from people who tend to suck you into unproductive conversations. At the very least, keep these conversations to time outside of the office or at lunch.

If legitimate work distractions take up a lot of your time, include them when you create a schedule for your day. That way, you'll know if you're wasting your time with useless tasks unrelated to work, or if your situation contributes to your lack of productivity. Use this information when you assess your priorities and calendar your time.

HOW TO TRACK YOUR TIME

Identify where you are wasting your time. Is your morning routine a little too casual, or do you have trouble getting anything done after lunch? Hone in on your most—and least—productive times. Log how much work you do, and when.

Luckily, there are a lot of apps for your smartphone to help you time and track how you spend your time. Fieldguide.gizmodo.com suggests trying the following apps: Hours, Jiffy, RescueTime, Toggl, Chronos, or ATracker.

You may prefer to write tasks down on paper or use websites designed to keep you on track, such as Basecamp, which allows you to see all of your assignments, update their status, and cross them off when finished.

Assess Your Priorities

Every day, take a deep breath (literally) and identify what needs to get done today (and what doesn't). You shouldn't make a list until you assess your priorities. Many people work in organizations where every item seems like a top priority. However, there is only so much one person can accomplish in a day. If that reminds you of your workplace, ask your supervisor for help ranking your priorities. If you don't have regular meetings, this might be a good way to help illustrate what you are managing at work. If it really is too much, perhaps your boss may reassign some of the work.

However, before you go to your boss for help, take a close look at how you spend your time at work. If you are distracted by work politics and gossiping in the elevator instead of checking off items on your "must do today" list, or spending too much time checking

Facebook or writing personal texts in the office when you could be working, make a change immediately. Bosses appreciate people who know how to manage their own time. Self assess before you ask for help and be as productive as you should be at work. (For more in-depth information about setting priorities, review Chapter 9.)

Track Your Work

Outline your projects and responsibilities. List them by day, and indicate how much time each item takes to complete. This exercise should help you assess where you may be wasting time. Write down everything you need to do and indicate how much time it takes. Try a time tracking app, such as Toggl. This app provides a timer and allows you to code items that take your time. Compare your plan with the actual amount of time, and determine where you are wasting time and where you have more time to shift to other tasks.

PROJECT	TIME NEEDED	ACTUAL TIME SPENT

Confer with Your Boss

The most successful people at work are able to anticipate and fulfill their boss' needs. When you make your boss look good, it inevitably helps you, too. What better way to learn to anticipate his or her needs than to know what's on his or her mind? Have priorities changed based on a new edict from above? Is something big coming up soon? What must you finish fast to make way for a new priority? Unless you're a mind reader, or have very good insider information, the only way to know what's important to your boss is to communicate with him or her.

If you don't already have regular meetings or check-ins, request additional communication, especially if you're having a tough time getting all of your work done or you have questions about how to prioritize your tasks.

Confer with Your Colleagues

If you're feeling overwhelmed at work, it's likely you're not the only one. Speak to your colleagues. Resist the urge to complain or to try to convince everyone you are so much busier than everyone else. Instead, learn how other people manage their work. Is anyone else having a tough time balancing the workload? What strategies do your colleagues use to get everything done on time? Perhaps you can identify a mentor or work buddy to help keep you on track and motivated. Is there someone whose work ethic and output you admire? What can you learn from him or her? Your professional future depends on knowing how to prioritize and finish quality assignments on time. Plan accordingly, and seek help if you need it.

BALANCE YOUR ROCKS AND PEBBLES

Have you heard the story about a speaker who went to the front of the room and put a big jar on the table, along with a bucket of sand, several large rocks, and pebbles? He told everyone they needed to fit everything in the jar. The moral of the story is the rocks (representing big projects) needed to go in the jar first, and the rest of the smaller pebbles and sand fit around it. When you prioritize the "big rocks," the most important things you need to get done, you'll have an easier time fitting everything into your busy workday.

Make a List

Whenever you have a growing list of tasks you must complete, rank jobs in order of importance. Indicate a realistic amount of time you expect each item to take, and note if you need to coordinate or collaborate with someone to finalize each item. The tasks that must get done today should be at the top of the list. Further down the list, include the carryover items you haven't finished from the day before. If you're in a situation where you can delegate some items, mark items you should delegate. Don't forget to include meetings or other events that require your attention during the day, as well as schedule lunch breaks.

Exercise: Make your list. Decide what type of list template works for you, or use this version:

To Do Today
In order of importance

_____

_____

_____

_____

_____

To Do This Week
In order of importance

_____

_____

_____

_____

_____

Longer Term To-Do List
In order of importance

_____

_____

_____

_____

_____

_____

Best List Features

In an article for Inc.com, Belle Beth Cooper, content crafter at Buffer (a tool to help schedule social media posts), suggests several ways to help make your work to-do list more useful. (Review Chapter 7 for an in-depth review of how to create lists to help you manage all of your priorities.)

- **Identify the toughest tasks.** If they need to get done today, do them first, while you are fresh and most productive.
- **Chunk it down.** Break down big projects or tasks into sections so they don't seem so overwhelming. When you segment projects, it's easier to identify how long each task actually takes.
- **Look for ways to be more productive.** What on your list is taking a lot longer than you thought it would? Try to identify why. Are you spending too much time trying to figure something out when you should simply ask a colleague a clarifying question? Are you redoing tasks someone else on the team already did? Look for ways to reduce the amount of time it will take you to complete your list. Is there anyone else handling similar tasks? Try to find out how long it takes that person to complete the same work. That way, you'll have a benchmark to gauge how long it should take you.
- **Create a "done" list.** Cooper suggests you complete a "running log of everything you complete in a day." It's a good way to track what you're doing and to hold yourself accountable. If you keep and review your lists and notice you become more or less productive, you can adjust your workflow accordingly. If you're interested in an app to help track and share this information, check out the iDoneThis app.

Another trick to help you with your workload is to accomplish some quick tasks if you know you're feeling tired or aren't at your best. Do the easy work at times when your energy lags and you'll be able to check items off your list.

BACK UP YOUR WORK

There are few things that will set you back more than losing your work after a computer glitch. Back up everything you do. Hopefully, your employer provides a way to save backups easily, especially if there are security or privacy issues surrounding your work. If not, and if you don't need to worry about security, keep your own backups on external drives or in the cloud. Alternatively, consider emailing yourself a copy of your materials as a backup.

Manage Your Email

Despite proclamations saying "email is dead," clearly it is alive and well, as likely evidenced by your inbox—which is probably over-flowing. Nothing will change with your overwhelming email unless you take significant steps to manage it.

No matter what email you use, sort and file it in easy to identify folders instead of letting it pile up in your inbox. Delete messages you don't need or that you realistically will never review again. Keep items you may want to use as proof of instructions or details. Save emails approving vacations, for example. If you have any personal messages in your work account (which is a big no-no), delete them. Tap into any filtering systems your email provides. If you don't know how to use them, ask someone who does. You may be able to sort and filter messages based on subject or content. Set this up once and tweak it as you go to be more efficient when you manage your email.

If possible (as long as it is allowed at your workplace), consider accessing an application to help manage your email. One application to try is called Boomerang (for Gmail or Outlook). The app allows you to write emails to schedule for later, choose to get reminders if no one replies to you, or remove messages in your inbox until you need them. This can be helpful to avoid forgetting emails when you're on the go.

Make sure you identify time on your to-do list to review email. Whether you do it at the beginning, middle, or end of your day, or you need more frequent blocks to manage incoming messages, set aside specific time to read and respond to your emails instead of interrupting yourself throughout the day. Some people advise you to avoid reviewing email first thing in the morning. For many, that seems unrealistic at best, or foolish at worst. Reading email is a way to find out what your day may have in store for you. However, you don't want to get bogged down with email first thing in the morning. If you do read emails in the morning, make it a point to take quick action or only read the most relevant messages.

Check Voicemail and Texts

If you hate voicemail, you're not alone. Many view it as an unwelcome interruption, and it's sometimes challenging to accurately transcribe messages with specific details. Don't check your voicemails unless you're in a place where you can hear the message and you're prepared to transcribe the contents. Otherwise, you risk forgetting the specifics or not following through on important tasks. If possible, encourage people to send emails or texts with detailed information instead.

Use the same rules for reviewing work related texts as you do voicemails. If you have a tendency to get busy and forget details, don't check your work texts on the go unless you have a plan in place to follow up. One idea is to always review your viewed texts at the end of each day. If you make it a habit, you won't lose any important information.

Your Calendar

An age-old tool, your calendar is your lifeline at work. Whether you swear by your paper day planner or embrace an online calendar, use it to write down all of your meetings, appointments, and deadlines. Include blocks for breaks and lunch. Set alerts in advance if you have long-term deadlines that you're tracking. For example, that report due a month from now may find places on your calendar every Monday, Wednesday, and Friday between now and the deadline so you're sure to make time to complete it. If you use an online calendar, set alerts or alarms to prompt you to take action at the right times. (Alternatively, you can use a paper calendar, but choose an alarm app for your smartphone for reminders.)

Only include a realistic amount of activities that you can complete during any given work day. You don't want to rush through your to-do list just to keep up. Provide reasonable and ample time to finish all of your work to your satisfaction, and schedule appointments with yourself, too. Depending on how busy you are, you may need to schedule time to eat, exercise, and socialize. For example, include downtime in your calendar, and include breaks, even if they're short.

Take Your Lunch

When you're scheduling your downtime, don't forget about lunch. Taking a break during the day can be good for your productivity. In an article for *Fast Company*, Rich Bellis quoted researcher Josh Davis, who said "If you want to solve a particularly difficult problem, letting your mind wander by engaging in an unrelated and cognitively easy task can help you find some creative solutions to that problem."

In his article, Bellis suggests the following ways to unwind during lunch.

Nap

Some companies have nap rooms, or you may be lucky enough to have an office with a door and a couch. A power nap can help refocus your attention and help you be a better problem solver. Realistically, this option isn't available for everyone at work, but luckily, there are other ways to take a break.

Get Some Exercise

Even if you can't run to the gym, you can take a brisk walk, either inside or outside. Even walking up and down stairs can get your blood moving. Bellis' article points out, "[A] key byproduct of exercise is BDNF, or 'brain-derived neurotrophic factor,' a protein that helps protect and repair parts of our mental infrastructure, including neurons involved in memory." You can get this benefit after only 20 minutes of exercise, so if you do have access to a gym and have an hour-long lunch break, you have plenty of time to exercise and shower.

Read

Bellis notes that reading, especially longer novels, can help benefit your brain. He writes, "Some studies have shown those who read regularly for pleasure have better planning, prioritizing, and decision-making skills than those who don't. There's also evidence that pleasure reading can help us cope with stress, anxiety, and depression, and subsequently to fend off illnesses like dementia." Luckily, most people should be able to easily access this mind break during the day. All you need is a quiet place and a little time to read and let your mind wander.

TAKE A NATURE BREAK

The Journal of Environmental Psychology details a 2015 Australian study that tested attention restoration—where microbreaks lasting under a minute can boost concentration.* Researchers concluded that looking at nature for as few as 40 seconds can help you improve your work performance. If possible, try to create your own microbreaks. Get up and find a window if necessary. Perhaps spending some time viewing nature can help you concentrate.

---

*www.medicalnewstoday.com/articles/294382.php

Avoid Multitasking

Most everyone tries to multitask. We watch television while balancing the checkbook or talking on the phone while typing emails. However innocent it seems, research from Stanford University* found that people who multitask are unable to really pay attention, control their memory, or shift between two jobs as well as those who complete one thing at a time. Eric Doland, writing on unclutterer.com, referenced Princeton University Neuroscience Institute's research that found a cluttered environment contributes to a chaotic environment, which restricts your ability to focus and limits the brain's ability to process information.

Brenna Loury, head of marketing at Todoist (a list and task manager), wrote a blog post about why you shouldn't multitask (https://blog.todoist.com/2014/05/13/how-multitasking-slows-your-brain-and-kills-your-productivity/). She notes that multitasking significantly reduces productivity, and points out that the

---

*http://news.stanford.edu/news/2009/august24/multitask-research-study-082409.html

cognitive functions of our brains cannot effectively switch between tasks. Writing for *Fast Company*, Kermit Pattison explains another risk of multitasking: Research suggests that if you switch from one task to another it takes an average of 23 minutes and 15 seconds to reset yourself to accomplish the original task. Loury says that multitasking ". . . actually reduces your productivity by a whopping 40% . . . and can lower your IQ by 10 points."

Trying to do multiple things simultaneously slows you down, and it's frightening to realize that doing so may also affect a multitasker's brain. Multitasking makes you less efficient, and likely results in sacrificing quality output in both tasks.

Don't make a mistake at work because you're trying to do too much. Instead, plot out your time efficiently and schedule hours for your work based on priorities. The upside of working this way? If you really do have too much work to accomplish in the allotted time, it will be easy for you to explain and illustrate the situation for your boss or co-workers if necessary.

Loury suggests the following methods to avoid the trap of multitasking:

- **The Pomodoro productivity method.** If you subscribe to this method, you'll work on one thing for a specific amount of time before you take a break. Track the number of times you are distracted while you are working and try to reduce those distractions during your next session. (Read more about this and other methods to plan your time in Chapter 9.)
- **Tap technology available to you.** Install an app, such as Inbox Pause for Gmail to decide when your emails will show up in your inbox. You can also try Anti-social. This program for Apple and Windows blocks websites for a specified amount of time, and you cannot undo the setting.
- **Don't try to work when you're tired.** When you schedule your tasks to synch with your most productive times, you're more likely to focus and not getting distracted.

In Summary: Action Tips

Plan your work and work your plan. Keep these tips in mind to have a more productive and successful day—every day.

- Incorporate healthy routines. Eat a good breakfast and exercise.
- Arrive early and arrange your day to be as productive as possible. This includes arranging your workspace so you can find everything and eliminating extra papers and trash you do not need.
- Manage distractions as best you can. Avoid getting caught gossiping at the water cooler and focus on your to-do list.
- Assess your priorities and track your work to make sure you are accomplishing important tasks. Keep in touch with your boss and your colleagues to be sure everyone knows what you're doing and how you're doing it.
- Keep long- and short-term lists and use your lists to help identify what to do next.
- Back up all your computerized work.
- Track emails, voicemails, and texts.
- Create a detailed calendar and use it.
- Take carefully planned and regimented breaks.
- Track your time and don't multitask.

6 Ending Your Work Day

How you end your workday is as important as how you begin it. Just as the most successful people begin their days strategically, they also end their day on the same note. Luckily, once you create a great process to manage your affairs at work, it's a lot easier to wrap up and start again. Read on to learn about the steps you should take at the end of each workday to ensure you don't have any gaps in your work life.

A productive day tomorrow starts by ending today on task and organized. Incorporate these items in your end-of-day routine and you can leave work confident your next day will be all set up and ready to go.

Review Email and Voicemail

Don't leave any messages unseen overnight. You'll want to know if there are any emergencies facing you in the near future or if anyone is expecting information from you anytime soon. Plus, if you clear your inbox (or, at least review what's there), listen to your voicemail messages, and review texts before you leave work, you can start fresh in the morning and not be behind the proverbial eight ball.

Finish Up Holdovers

If you're waiting to hear from someone or you can quickly address something that's hanging over on your to-do list, consider following up before another night passes. Also, when you give people updates on your progress, they're more likely to be allies with you in getting the job done. Try to eliminate items you carry on your list from one day to the next. If you notice you regularly pull items on your list from one day to another, consider why that happens. Should you send a friendly reminder to people who need to provide information for you at midday? Are you simply low on their priority lists? Perhaps you need to escalate the situation and engage a higher-up member of the team to help you access information. If you can prevent wasting a lot of time chasing people down for details you need to do your work with a few well-timed reminders, be sure do add this to your to-do list.

Make a To-Do List

This is your list for tomorrow to set the tone for the day to come. Pay special attention to anything you need to address before you come to work tomorrow including loose ends you couldn't finish before you left today. Use your existing list to create your next-day list and include overflow time if necessary, in case you need extra time to finish something.

When creating your list, follow priority order and indicate timeframes for each item. Be flexible in case something comes up at the last minute—leave breathing room for each task in case you get distracted or in case the activity takes longer than you think it will. If you encounter unexpected challenges, it will be easier to manage your list if you update it throughout the day.

Also, if you have a meeting in the morning, set aside everything you need before you leave work so you won't need to look for anything when you arrive in the morning.

Before you create your next day's list, evaluate your general progress at the end of the day with your current list. Are you making progress on the tasks you need to finish? Did you check off most of your items for the day? If not, be sure you know why not. If it's because an unexpected emergency called you from the office or you needed to jump in to help a colleague with something, move on and try to get them done the next day. If there is no reason you shouldn't have accomplished everything on your to-do list, identify the reasons why you didn't finish. Then, alter your habits accordingly. Take careful notes—if you regularly have unexpected things added to your to-do list throughout any given day, you should start planning for them in your lists.

This is a sample to-do list to create the night before. You don't actually need to list "get coffee" on your to-do list on a daily basis, and you aren't likely to take the time daily to write a list that specifies the time to walk to and from a meeting. However, this list is comprehensive, to give you an idea of items you may want to include, especially when you're tracking your time and evaluating where all your time goes during the day. (See Chapter 7 for more tips on creating productive and efficient lists.)

8:15–8:30: Arrive at work. Get coffee, check emails, and make notes of anything new since night before.

8:30–8:45: Mentally prepare for the day and collect all paperwork necessary for 9:00 meeting.

8:45–9:00: Walk with team to meeting down the street.

9:00–10:30: Meeting

10:30–10:45: Walk back to work.

10:45–11:00: Debrief meeting with team and write down action steps.

11:00–12:00: Work on XYZ project. (Make a new list of people to contact, research at least five contacts, and compile email for new contacts.)

12:00–1:00: Mental break and lunch. Try to include a 20-minute walk outside. Get away from desk and screens.

1:00–1:30: Buffer time to finish anything hanging over from yesterday or today and address new tasks from meeting.

1:30–2:30: Work on ABC project. (Create new database fields, test new output, and print out results.)

2:30–3:30: Put up "do not disturb sign" and list out strategies for next steps for ABC project.

3:30–3:45: Buffer time to make personal phone calls, look at personal emails, and get a quick work task done. (If you schedule this time, you're less likely to waste a lot of time getting them done throughout the day. This assumes you have flexibility in your day to handle some personal things.)

3:45–5:00: Time to be available to touch base with team members to discuss XYZ and ABC projects. (List problems you need to address or issues to solve during this time.)

5:00–5:15: Wind down and plan for tomorrow. List accomplishments for brag list, if appropriate. Collect materials needed for tomorrow's meetings and make sure everything is finished that is required for the beginning of the next day.

Savor Your Wins

Did you accomplish something big today? Add it to your brag list. You don't have a brag list? It's time to start one! Don't rely on your memory when it comes to listing and classifying your accomplishments. Take these steps to help document information that may help you land a new job or promotion in the future. At least once a week, be sure to document any accomplishments you want to remember.

Create a Place to Document Accomplishments

Some people put their brag list information on their work computer in a folder, using basic tools such as Excel or Word. For example, you may make a simple list of things you got done. If you're lucky, you can document notes from clients or supervisors thanking you for something you did well. You may want to keep an email folder of these nice notes. If you do that, you should also back them up on a separate, accessible computer or application. Some tools to try to document your accomplishments include: Evernote, WorkSmart, and www.goalsontrack.com.

If you're creative, you may want to maintain a digital portfolio. LinkedIn is an obvious place to start. You can add your major accomplishments easily to your profile. In addition, consider using Flavors.me or About.me to create a digital profile you can easily update and share. If you're very motivated and technologically savvy (or know someone who is), you may want to start a social resume on your own professional website. Reserve YourName.com and create a portfolio site where you can easily add content, documents, and relevant links.

Start a Physical Folder

If you're old fashioned and not inclined to digitize everything, set up a folder or box where you keep paper files or notes from clients or happy customers, as well as written details you'll want to remember in the future about certain accomplishments.

Note Specifics about Your Wins

While you may not have time at the end of a busy day to start documenting all of the details, make time to note key information you'd need to update your resume. For example, include metrics (such as dollar figures, revenues, percent increases, budget information, comparisons to expectations, time saved, etc.). You'll want all of this information at a later date, so don't let too much time go by before you compile it—you don't want to forget about major accomplishments if too much time passes before you get a chance to update your paperwork!

Plan to Ask a Supervisor for a Recommendation on LinkedIn

It's not necessarily something you'll do the minute your accomplishment is evident, but within a week or so, ask your boss to acknowledge and document your win (if strategically feasible). Put together the numbers and note as much information as you can about your role. Be specific, so your recommender can easily include details you want to be public.

Don't Hesitate to Share Great News via Your Social Media Platforms

As long as you're not constantly bragging about how great you (or your family members) are on Facebook or Twitter, your community will likely celebrate a share-worthy win. While this may be a good way to share news, it's not necessarily the best way to track your accomplishments, so be sure you do another item on this list in addition to sharing on social media.

Exercise: Create a Brag List

You haven't been carefully tracking and recording contributions you make at work? How are you going to create a detailed resume and prepare to discuss your skills and accomplishments? Do not delay—start now and document your professional wins. If necessary, review a copy of your resume and add in notes about your best accomplishments. Include everything you remember, such as specific numbers (money saved, money made, percent improvements, year-over-year, etc.). If you won awards you never included in your resume, add them now. It's probably a challenge to remember all of this important information. Commit to tracking these details going forward.

_____

_____

_____

_____

_____

_____

_____

_____

_____

_____

_____

_____

_____

END-OF-DAY PRODUCTIVITY TIPS FROM PROFESSIONALS

Karen Dobkin, CPA, explains how she ends her workday:

If I can't get my to-do list completed by the end of the day, and someone is expecting something from me, I send a note to apologize for the delay. My clients appreciate hearing from me and recognize I value and appreciate them. I also make a point to send confirmation emails for appointments the next day. This is another habit that helps everyone use their time well and avoids last-minute misunderstandings.

Preschool teacher Rebecca Blau suggested:

Without staying too late, try to do one task you would normally do the next day. If you do this every day, you'll always be ahead of your workload and you'll also leave feeling like your productivity game is on point.

Kathy Mathews, educator and writer, advises:

At the end of the day, remember to thank everyone who helped you, either via email, a quick written note, or by saying thank you on your way out. Always identify ways you could do your job better the next day, too. For example, if you gave a presentation or lecture, write down how to improve it next time. Update your handouts or informational emails with new information so they'll be ready to use. Finally, take pictures of any product you may have created to use as a model for next time.

Barbara Marks, a talent acquisition professional, reminds people who want to reorganize their workdays to pick tips that seem most likely to help and then stick with them for three weeks or longer. She notes:

When people who have trouble managing their workloads try to make changes, they often fail because they are not consistent in how they apply tools and techniques to improve their workflow. Trying one technique one week and a different technique the following week doesn't provide enough time to succeed.

Take Responsibility for What You Didn't Finish

What items have been dragging along week after week on your to-do list? Why aren't you checking them off? Whether the hold up is strictly your fault or you can share the blame with someone who hasn't gotten back to you, assume it is your responsibility to address the lagging item. Make a point to take care of it as a priority the next day, or remove it from the list if it is not important enough to address.

Touch Base with Your Boss and Colleagues

Ask what you want to know. Find out everyone else's work status, especially as it relates to you. If you're waiting for something, find out when you can expect it and identify new or updated deadlines.

Check the Calendar

There's nothing worse than forgetting an early-morning meeting or forgetting about a special guest you're expecting the next day. Always check your calendar at the end of each workday so you won't have any surprises in the morning.

Clean Up Your Work Area

Are you so busy you didn't even recycle the soda can on your desk? Are papers piling up so much they may fall off your desk? Do wrappers dangle gracefully off the back of your desk? Throw away your garbage and get organized. Just as you cleared your digital space (email, voicemails, and texts), you should leave your physical space in order. If you spend a few minutes at the end of every day tidying up your things, you can save a lot of time later. Not only will you prevent unwanted and unnecessary papers from taking over your work space, you'll present an organized appearance to your colleagues, most of whom will assume a cluttered desk is the sign of a cluttered mind. (Review Chapter 10 for more advice about how important it is to straighten up your work area.)

Do Something Nice and Say Goodbye

Whether it's setting up the coffee pot for the next day, adding paper or toner to the printer, or something else more personal to help a colleague, helping someone else is a great way to end your day. If you're always stressed out and running out the door, consider making time to do this at least once a week. It might help brighten your day to end it by helping someone else.

Don't slink out of the office. Give your colleagues a friendly goodbye greeting to help end the day on a positive note. Make a special effort to touch base with anyone who went out of their way to help you, as well as with colleagues with whom you may have had a tense moment. It's easier to start the next day if you finish up with a kind word and a good wish.

What NOT to Do at the End of the Day

Do you need a to-do and a not to-do list? Here are some helpful reminders of things not to add to the end of your day.

Don't Start Something New

Even if you notice a new project or assignment, if you're getting ready to close your computer and walk out the door, don't begin a new project at the end of the day. Add the information to your to-do list for the next work day.

Don't Send Off Rushed Emails or Texts

It isn't ideal to communicate in writing when you're in a hurry. Inevitably, you'll make careless errors or adopt a tone your audience may misinterpret. Or worse, you may accidentally "Reply all" when your message is only for one person. Unless there is an emergency, wait until the next day, after you've had a chance to consider your reply. Instead, add the item to your list and end your day.

Don't Make a Big Decision or Work on Something That Takes More Energy than You Have

You know your own energy level and ability to concentrate. If you tend to feel like you are dragging at the end of the day, avoid committing to any key decisions and don't work on projects that are detail oriented or otherwise very involved right at the end of the day. Save this work for when you are more rested in the morning. Add the items to your morning to-do list before you leave.

Don't Bring Your Work (and Your Stress) Home

For some people, this may not be realistic advice. However, no matter how busy or involved your job is, make an effort to disconnect to the extent you reasonably can at the end of the day. Give yourself a break and you'll be better prepared to get back to work the next day.

Exercise: End-of-Day Checklist

Use the information suggested in this chapter to create a personalized, end-of-day checklist. What do you need to do before you leave work that isn't mentioned here? What reminders will help you end your day on a good note? Be intentional each day about checking off items on your list, and you'll set yourself up for a better day tomorrow.

_____

_____

_____

_____

_____

_____

_____

_____

_____

_____

_____

_____

_____

_____

_____

In Summary: Action Tips

End your day and prepare for the next one using these tips:

- Finish up loose ends and review any messages (email, text, or voice) before you leave work. Finish up anything you've been holding over all day long so you don't need to start it again in the morning.
- Make formal notes of any wins you want to remember for the long term.
- Take responsibility for what you didn't finish and connect with your boss and colleagues if necessary.
- Check the calendar so you know what's happening tomorrow.
- Clean up before you leave work, and try to do something nice for a colleague.
- Say goodbye; don't slink out of the office.
- Don't start anything new when you're about to leave, and don't send rushed messages out or make decisions you haven't thought out.
- Avoid bringing your work stress home with you.

III

HOW TO MAINTAIN AN ORGANIZED WORK AND HOME LIFE

7

Using Lists to Be More Efficient

No matter what task you're tackling, from grocery shopping to job search to working efficiently so you accomplish your big goals, your first step is to create an effective to-do list. Make it easy on yourself by using a tool you enjoy that's easy for you to update frequently. If you're a traditionalist, a handwritten checklist may appeal to you, although it may be more difficult to update it neatly. Others who prefer more low-tech methods may type lists and easily add or change them on their computers. For the more technologically inclined, there are a myriad of applications and tools to use to maintain lists. Some even help coordinate lists or projects between people, which can come in handy if you're working with other people on some of your job search items.

If you really want to make the most of your to-do lists, follow these tips and you'll benefit from a more efficient, effective process.

Keep Multiple Lists

Best practices for list making suggest that you break up your lists into several versions. For example, a short-term list of things will include items you want to do today or in the next few days. Another list may include items you plan for the future. Perhaps you'll keep a running list of things you're planning to accomplish this week or this month. If you're really list savvy, you'll create all of these types of lists and plan your steps methodically so you can check off items every day. If you do, it's more likely you'll follow through and complete all of the steps you must accomplish to keep your plans consistently moving forward.

When you break up your lists, you won't constantly be faced with a huge group of items that may overwhelm you. If you're overwhelmed, you're more likely to flee from your list than you are to methodically check things off.

Compile Master Lists

Make lists that make sense to you. Many people find that breaking down lists by goals is helpful. For example, your first list might be a master list of everything you need to do for your job search. This will be a long list, and should include a lot of the items explained in this book. This "master" list could include basic building block items. If you're planning a job hunt for example, items on your master list may include:

- Create a list of my own skills.
- Identify companies where I'd like to work.
- Match my skills sets and list of accomplishments to job descriptions.
- Create a resume that details skills, accomplishments, and results.

- Identify people in my network who may be able to provide insights or information.
- Create introductory email messages to connect with people.
- Find networking events to attend.

Each of these items could have several sub-items under it. For example, under "Create a list of my own skills," you may add steps to help you do that, such as:

- Review past performance reviews.
- Look over current and past job descriptions.
- Ask people what they think my skills include.

Reviewing a long, drawn out list can be intimidating. However, when you have a comprehensive list, it's easier to hold yourself accountable for each step of your plan. Consider creating a master list that includes every step you need to accomplish for a specific topic.

Break Down Your List

Once you create an in-depth list, you can break it down into a smaller, more manageable list of things you know you can accomplish in certain periods of time. For example:

- Create a list of my own skills by (*date*).
- Review my existing resume.
- Look at job descriptions of positions I held in the past.
- Review job descriptions of positions I can see myself doing.
- Look over recommendations and performance reviews written about me.
- Ask people who are familiar with my work what they think are my best skills.

If you work diligently, you should be able to finish all of these tasks within a week or two weeks, at the most (except talking to people, since you'll need to schedule times to meet with them). If you prefer, break the list down into daily tasks and track your progress that way.

Compile a Punch-Out List

You may also want to keep a punch-out list. This would include easy tasks to help propel your plans forward. Punch-outs are for those items that don't require a lot of preparation. Sticking with our job search example, this list would include names and numbers of people you need to call who are easy for you to reach or who don't require much planning before you speak to them. Since these calls are easy to accomplish, these names go on your punch-out list. Your former boss, who is also a good friend, might be a good candidate for this list if it is easy to chat with her and ask about what skills she thinks you have, for example. You don't need to create scripts to speak to someone on your punch-out list. These items are perfect to accomplish when you're too tired to complete the tougher items. If you keep this type of list, you'll never have an excuse to take time off from moving your job search ahead.

Write Down Your Must-Do List

Without overwhelming yourself with lists, consider having a must-do list. This is a little different from a punch-out list, because they aren't necessarily the easiest items; it includes the things you *need* to do before accomplishing something else. For example, if you have a meeting with a networking contact on Friday, you must prepare for the meeting and create a list of questions (or whatever you need to create) by Thursday night at the latest. Make sure you give yourself enough time to prepare; otherwise, you risk wasting an opportunity to learn what you need to know at the meeting.

INCLUDE DETAILS IN YOUR LISTS

If you really want to leverage your lists, make sure they include everything you need to do and everything you need to know. It sounds time consuming to create detailed lists, but if you follow through on a daily basis, you may find it helpful to have all the necessary details written down. For example, if you need to email someone, include that person's email address. Don't put yourself in the position of sitting down with your list, only to have to start digging up information in order to accomplish the tasks. Part of making the list should be doing the legwork necessary to actually accomplish each item on the list.

Estimate Timeframes and Always Include Them

What if you have an hour free? Wouldn't it be great if you could review your list and find something you can accomplish in one hour? Give yourself time slots in which to accomplish each task, to encourage you to be more accountable and help you move through your list in a timely way. Plus, if you know something will take hours and hours to do, not only can you break it into manageable parts, you can give yourself realistic deadlines and plan your time so nothing slips through the cracks.

Share Your List

Could you benefit from accountability? Do you need to post your to-do list on the refrigerator at home, or share pieces of it via social media or through apps? If you have a friend who is also looking for a job, perhaps the two of you can compare notes or check in on each other. You obviously don't want someone to nag you, but it can't hurt to have a friend in your corner, helping make sure you aren't wasting time when you could be making your way through your job search to-do list.

Avoid These To-Do List Mistakes

Hopefully, quality to-do lists will help you track what you need to do each day. Avoid these common mistakes to prevent to-do list pitfalls that can thwart your efforts.

Don't Forget to Prioritize

Assign a priority level to each item you need to address. Ideally, priority items are at the top of your list. Always take care of the most timely and pressing items first, and move through your list from the top to the bottom.

Don't Be a Check-Off Fiend

It's great to check things off your list, but avoid checking items off prematurely just to have something checked for the day. Quality is more important than quantity when it comes to your professional life. If your lists are so onerous that you can't ever accomplish something well enough to check it off, revise your lists. Break them into smaller, more manageable pieces so you can get that feeling of accomplishment that comes from putting a check on your list—without sacrificing a job well done.

Don't Save Least-Favorite Tasks for Last

It's tempting to procrastinate and hold the tasks you dislike for the very end of your list. However, one best practice is to sometimes do things you don't enjoy first. That way, you won't have an unenviable item at the end of every list—or every day. Is there a call you dread making? Do it right away. Once you finish, you can check it off your list and move on to items you enjoy doing more.

Give Yourself Enough Down Time

It's tempting to schedule all of your time. After all, you're goal-oriented and need to make it through a lot of different lists if you want the best chance to be competitive. However, if you don't take breaks, you run the risk of burning out. Plus, if you're not scheduling breaks, you'll probably sneak them in while you're supposed to be getting other things done. The time you lose with unscheduled breaks adds up, and you might have been able to take a whole day off instead of lots of little, unscheduled breaks—if you'd been more conscientious.

Avoid Multitasking

It's tempting to try to do a lot of things at once. However, research shows our brains aren't set up to simultaneously handle a lot of items. When you're writing your networking list, don't constantly check your email or social media outlets. If you prevent distractions, including the television, noisy family rooms, and busy coffee shops, you'll give yourself the chance to successfully tackle your lists.

Learn from the Past

Don't doom yourself to the same poor results you may have had in the past, when you didn't manage your time and your lists well. If you know a particular item is going to take more time than you allotted because the last time you tried to finish a similar task it took longer than you'd expected, adjust your schedule accordingly.

Don't Go It Alone

Are you generally disorganized? Do you envy people who keep and follow lists, but you've never been someone who even made a list before grocery shopping because it felt too restrictive? Ask for help. If you don't think you're up for creating these types of short- and long-term lists, consider asking a well-organized friend to help, or hire a coach to help you make a plan and to keep you accountable.

SELECT THE BEST LIST-MAKING APPS FOR YOU

The Zapier.com blog lists 40 of their favorite to-do apps, broken down by category, such as:

- grocery list apps, which organize tasks in basic lists
- getting things done apps, which incorporate sub-lists and time management tools
- Kanban Board apps, which help you visualize your progress
- plain text apps and miscellaneous other applications to explore

Google their list, or ask your contacts for their favorite apps.

Before you dive into an app to help keep you on task, evaluate the experience you want and what, specifically, you'll want to track. Then, select one or two apps that might work for you and give them a trial period.

Exercise: Find Some Apps

Even if you think you prefer paper and pencil, extend yourself and find one or two productivity applications that suit your needs. Most are free or have free trials. Read about at least three that have features that would appeal to you and use each one for a few days. For example, you may want to find an app that builds in some accountability by sharing your list with other people who can check in on your progress. Or, you may surprise yourself and find you actually prefer to manage lists on your smart phone. Discover what tools and methods work best for you, and stick with them.

In Summary: Action Tips

When you learn how to use to-do lists to your advantage, you'll have a much easier time managing your time and your life efficiently. Follow these best practices to help make your lists as useful as possible.

- **Keep multiple lists.** Short- and long-term lists will help you focus on what you need to accomplish.
- **Keep lists that identify how much time each item on the list will take, and break down the lists by goals.** Don't over-schedule your time, and do remember to incorporate breaks and down time. Include the building blocks you need to accomplish before you accomplish each larger goal in your list, and check off each one as you make progress.
- **Keep a punch out list.** This includes the easy items you need to do. Refer to it when you have extra time so you can use that time efficiently.
- **Write a must-do list.** What do you need to do first before accomplishing other tasks? Those items go on your must-do list.

- **Share your lists.** Will accountability help you accomplish your tasks? Share your to-do lists with friends or colleagues who are willing to help you keep up with your work. Don't go it alone!
- **Avoid mistakes.** Prioritize, and don't check items off your list until they're completely finished. Remember: quality is more important than quantity. Don't move too quickly and get sub-par results. Give yourself down time, and avoid multi-tasking.
- **Tap into technology.** Explore available technology and applications to help you accomplish more in less time, and to track what you need to do next.

CHAPTER

8

Tracking and Planning Your Long-Term Milestones and Short-Term Deadlines

Realistically, it's impossible to map out your long-term future and your entire life accurately. There are too many unknowns and changing factors to prepare for all possible scenarios. However, failing to plan isn't a good option, either. How can you prepare for an uncertain future? Consider what you want—or need—from your home and work life. Ask yourself what steps you can take right now to plot out and accomplish your goals. The saying "A goal is a dream with a deadline," is true. You can turn your dreams into accomplishments by setting goals and marking deadlines.

While you plan for the future, it's important to pay attention to near-term goals, too. Mapping out milestones using short- and long-term outlooks will pay off for your career success.

Identify Long-Term Milestones

In an article for *Forbes*,* Paul Brown, co-author (with Leonard A. Schlesinger and Charles F. Kiefer) of *Just Start: Take Action; Embrace Uncertainty and Create the Future*, acknowledges you can't predict the future several years out. In some cases, it is difficult to plan for the next month. In other words, you cannot control the economy, your workplace, or even your family. However, you do know what is important to you. Brown suggests you plan your life and prepare for professional opportunities by asking yourself who you are and what you value. What matters in your life, whether it is personal or professional? What do you need to accomplish the life you want to live?

Those are far-reaching questions many people never stop to ask themselves. While you may not be able to finalize your answers during your commute—or even over the course of a week or a month—start thinking about mapping out a plan for your future now. The first step is to envision what you want your life to look like, whether it's one year from now or five years ahead.

Since we can't dissect ourselves into separate work and personal life pieces, include both personal and professional goals when you envision your future. Writing for *Inc.*,** Peter Economy, author of more than 75 books, including *Managing For Dummies*, *The Management Bible*, and *Leading Through Uncertainty*, suggests that you create a life map that includes "your accomplishments, your work, your personal relationships, your financial goals, and more." Don't limit yourself—*and more* is purposefully vague. What's important to you will differ significantly from what other people value. Maybe your goals include more time for family, opportunities to explore your personal passions

---

*www.forbes.com/sites/actiontrumpseverything/2013/01/13/how-to
-plan-your-life-when-you-cant-plan-your-life/
**www.inc.com/peter-economy/7-awesome-ways-to-map-out-your
-dream-job.html

(such as art or sports), or perhaps you want to start a non-profit organization or be promoted to head of your department.

Mapping out your future doesn't require you to build all of the paths to accomplish your goals today, but it does provide a road map to help ensure you're moving in the direction most likely to take you where you want to go. If you don't know where you're going, you'll never arrive. This is particularly true when it comes to life plans.

Create a Vision Board

Many people believe in the "Law of Attraction," which says you can attract positive or negative thoughts or ideas based on your focuses in life. In other words, if you imagine yourself succeeding, you are more likely to succeed.

How can you put that intangible thought into action? One step to help you visualize your goals is to create a vision board, a tool to help you visualize and focus on your future goals. Your vision board may be a physical object with pictures you cut out to put together, or it may be a digital vision board where you compile pictures, or even affirmations, online or right from your phone. In other words, instead of writing a list of things you'd like to accomplish, this activity engages you in a visual exercise and helps you visualize your future. A vision board may include pictures to represent places you'll live, such as a picture of a house you hope to own. It may also showcase pictures featuring your work and home lives. The sky is the limit, as your vision board can be as big and as broad as your imagination

Why should you consider using a vision board to jumpstart your plans? Wellness expert Elizabeth Rider wrote about vision boards for *The Huffington Post*.* She explained, "Visualization is one of the

---

*www.huffingtonpost.com/elizabeth-rider/the-scientific-reason-why_b_6392274.html

most powerful mind exercises you can do." Rider points out that athletes have long relied on visualization to improve their results. She notes, "*Psychology Today* reported that the brain patterns activated when a weightlifter lifts heavy weights are also similarly activated when the lifter just imagined (visualized) lifting weights." In other words, "Whether you believe that or not, we know that visualization works."

Do you need some ideas to start your vision board? Consider selecting pictures capturing your dreams regarding your career, personal life (including family, love life, and friends), educational goals, where you want to live, places you hope to visit, and people you'd like to meet. Dream big and incorporate pictures and images of what you'd like your life to be in the future. Experts advise you include images of what you hope to have and things you enjoy, as well as how you want to feel. Add inspirational quotes or thoughts to your vision board, too. Be sure to keep your board neat. You don't want to invite chaos into your life, so focus it on your key goals, and images and words that best represent your future.

Once you create your vision board, you should keep it in a place where you'll see it often and refer to the images you created. Allow yourself some time each day or night to reflect on your visions and the steps needed to accomplish them. For example, if you included a picture of a diploma on your vision board to represent a degree you hope to earn, consider what you should put on your daily or monthly to-do list in order to set yourself up to earn your degree.

Exercise: Create Your Vision Board

Are you inspired by the idea of creating a pictorial of your future? Perhaps you welcome the opportunity to use scissors and a glue stick to put together something to help inspire you. Maybe you'd prefer to tap a smart phone app to help plan your future. Even if you're not convinced it will help you accomplish your goals, put something together to help you navigate towards your chosen future.

As noted, your vision board can be high tech or old school. For example, you may sit down with a pile of magazines and tear out pictures of things that represent your future. Alternatively, you can use a tool such as Pinterest to collect and create boards that represent things you like or want. Pinterest users post everything from images with inspirational quotes to pictures of homes or shoes, and everything in between. You can search within Pinterest for images you like and "pin" them to your online board. Alternatively, you may want to try using some vision board apps for your mobile device. Visit http://makeavisionboard.com/vision-board-apps/ for several ideas to get you started.

Write Down Steps to Accomplish Your Long-Term Plans

Your vision board is your reminder of what you want to accomplish in life and at work. Once you have visual goals, it's much easier to put the steps in place to ensure you accomplish your goals. Ask yourself, "What do I need to do to achieve these plans?" Segment your goals into categories, for example: work, home, personal, and education.

You have a lot of power to make a change for the better. If you want to change jobs, for example, you'll need to list what skills you must have to land the new job. If you don't already have those skills, include notes and details describing how you plan to learn them. Create in-depth lists to help accomplish your long-term plans. Then, take steps forward to make your goals a reality.

Break It Down
Don't allow yourself to be overwhelmed by long-term plans. Think about the steps you'll take to accomplish each goal, and group

them by category. Depending on your goals, you may even want to group things by date. For example, if you want to accomplish three things in the next six months, list them together and indicate steps you'll take to reach each goal. You may want to create a mind map, which is a visual representation of non-linear plans, to help you envision your plans and the steps needed to reach them.

Create a Mind Map

Especially if you're a visual learner or thinker, a mind map can help you plan your future goals. Whether you create your mind map using paper and pen, or you rely on an application or software to help flesh out your plan, these graphical tools, which may be color coded and include images, words, or both, provide an overview of your plans and help you create associations between one goal to the next. A mind map can help you realize if you are forgetting key steps needed to achieve your long-term goals.

Tony Buzan, host of a BBC television series, popularized the term mind map and suggested the following guidelines to create them:

- Put an image representing the topic in the center of your map, and select at least three colors to incorporate.
- Identify images and symbols to incorporate in the mind map.
- Choose key words to include. Every word or image should have its own space on your mind map.
- Connect the different sections of your map to the central image. Lines should all start from the center and radiate out.
- Make the lines the same length as the word/image they support.
- Group topics and ideas with similar colors or images.
- Be creative. Create something that will inspire you.

These suggestions will be particularly helpful if you're starting your mind map using paper and pen. However, you can also leverage one of the many applications that will handle the visual piece of your mind map for you. All you need to do is enter the information you need mapped.

Exercise: **Create a Mind Map**

Try your hand at creating a mind map and plotting out your goals. Consider what you want to accomplish and what steps you must take to reach those goals. Think about the accomplishments that led you to where you are today. List them, and use them to help you decide what you need to map out for the future. Write down every goal. Include new skills you want to learn, as well as job titles you're hoping to achieve or accomplishments you want to add.

For each goal, be sure to list the steps you need to take to reach it. For example, if you plan to earn a degree or certificate in the long term, your shorter-term goals should include researching programs, identifying financial resources (perhaps saving money), and meeting with people to discuss various programs. When you review your list, ask yourself what steps you may have missed when you outline the plans. Include additional in-between steps as necessary.

Educator Melisa Getzow outlined this mind map for someone thinking about purchasing a new car.

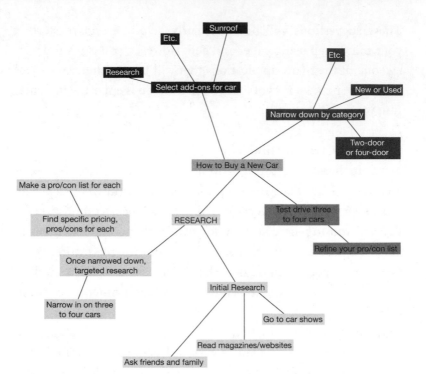

Consider trying a digital tool to create your visual plan. Try one of these or another of your choice:

- https://bubbl.us/mindmap
- www.xmind.net
- www.mindmup.com

How to Meet Short-Term Goals

Once you outline your long-term goals, fitting in short-term goals and tracking deadlines should be a little easier. Ultimately, all of your short-term goals lead to long-term goals, whether or not you outline all of them. In the near term, track deadlines to keep abreast of your calendar in order to successfully move forward.

Accomplish Deadlines

Deadlines are the small steps along the road to your success at work and in your personal life. When you plan your time to meet your deadlines and institute steps to prevent problems that would impede you from meeting your deadlines, you'll be well on your way to effectively managing your time and your life.

How to Manage Deadlines

The first step in meeting deadlines is to respect them as important milestones in your routine. At work and in your personal life, if people cannot count on you to follow through with your promises, you will have a difficult time earning their trust. If you've worked with someone who regularly misses deadlines, you know how disruptive it is. Make it a priority to focus on these key markers and to accomplish goals you set for yourself or that others provide you.

The first step in meeting these milestones is to understand them. Sometimes, people communicate poorly and do not clearly state when they need work completed. For example, if the deadline is "the end of the week," what does that mean? What if your boss (or a friend) says, "I'd like to have the information on Monday" or "Please get back to me on Monday"? Is Monday a firm deadline, or a suggestion? If you're operating under the impression that the guideline is a suggestion, but your boss or friend believes he's given you a deadline, you're asking for trouble.

Be clear and communicate specifically when discussing something that could be interpreted as a deadline. Ask questions if people use murky language or aren't explicit. For example, you could respond to a request for information on Monday with the inquiry, "Do you need to have this on Monday, or can I get back to you by Tuesday at 10 a.m.?" Note the specific request. If you try to clarify a deadline without asking for details, you could further confuse the situation.

BE FLEXIBLE

When it comes to deadlines, whether for work or in your personal life, be flexible. It may be aggravating when priorities shift in the middle of projects, but it's a fact of life in most workplaces and in your personal life, too. Adaptability is a much sought after skill in the workplace, so don't do or say anything to jeopardize your status as a flexible team player. Your best bet is to take everything in stride and not complain. When you plan your work, build in time for the unexpected and you'll be better equipped to handle changes on a moment's notice.

Another tip to help plan ahead: always get as much done as you possibly can at any given point in your work plan, even if the official deadline is far off. Since you never know what may happen between now and your actual deadline, do everything you can to get ahead of schedule. This approach also helps address personal concerns that may affect your work. If you get sick, or need to manage an unexpected situation at home, being ahead of schedule will help keep you from falling too far behind.

One way to always ensure you meet deadlines is by managing them to suit your schedule. While it isn't always possible (especially in a work environment) to control your deadlines, setting clear expectations you know you can meet is a big step toward hitting your targets and keeping people around you happy. Try to exercise control of deadlines imposed on you by negotiating them to suit your needs. If you know you won't be able to get a project, information, or email response to a colleague by a certain time, never say you will. Doing so will only put you in a position to disappoint your coworker, and you'll wind up apologizing later. Whenever possible, incorporate cushions into deadlines. For example, if you know you'll be able to deliver by October 15, but a deadline of October 22 is acceptable, ask for the later deadline and finish early. "Underpromise and overdeliver" is a mantra that may help you create an impression that you're reliable and meet your deadlines.

Understand Your Schedule

It's virtually impossible to negotiate a deadline you know you can manage unless you have a firm handle on your schedule. Track your projects and how much time you expect each to take. If you've followed advice from Chapter 7, you already track items you need to accomplish with a comprehensive list that includes how much time each item requires, so you should be well prepared to provide accurate, up-to-the-minute information about reasonable deadlines—so you can negotiate scenarios to suit your needs. Don't count on a disorganized calendar or your unreliable memory to keep up with deadlines. Implement a system to track your deadlines, whether it's a basic paper and pen calendar or a more sophisticated system that relies on applications to determine how much time you spend on various projects.

Ask for Help if Necessary

Realistically, you won't always be able to maneuver and adjust deadlines, but you should be prepared to discuss your workload and to ask for help if you need it. One caveat to keep in mind: Don't request help until you're *absolutely sure* you've done everything you can to manage your own schedule. Try to address the problem yourself first, and understand why you need help and exactly what would be most useful to you. For example, if you are handling two major projects, and you need assistance to keep up with the second project until you finish with the first, ask for that. Do you need tactical help or strategic help? Do you need another pair of hands, or someone to brainstorm better ways to do things?

Once you identify the type of help you need, you'll be able to decide on the best person to ask. You'll probably need to talk to your manager unless you only need a little extra boost, or a small amount of time or energy from a colleague. For example, you may want to request an adjusted deadline for another, less crucial project in order to take on something new. Or, perhaps there are items on your to-do list that you can reasonably pass along to someone else. If you've been too relaxed about keeping up with your to-do list and got behind as a result, you may want to consider putting in some extra hours to get caught up before you ask for help. Either way, it's best if you have some suggested solutions when you ask for help, instead of just a problem.

Don't allow yourself to be buried in work without requesting assistance; no one appreciates a martyr, especially one who doesn't accomplish goals. Identify potential solutions to help you manage your schedule. When you decide to ask for help, articulate what you've been doing to manage the project so far. Be clear about what you've already done and describe obstacles you've encountered. For example, perhaps you're spending a lot of time waiting to hear back from people, which is delaying the project. Someone with a higher level of authority may be able to help cut through this kind of red tape.

CONFIRM MEETINGS AND SEND REMINDERS

One aspect of meeting deadlines, both in personal and professional contexts, is addressing people who do not hold up their ends of the bargain and cause delays in your schedule. While you can't control other people and force them to maintain deadlines, you can help them along the way, which could result in a lot less aggravation for you.

Don't waste your time being stood up at a meeting. Whether it's your best friend who forgot about meeting for coffee or a work colleague who is late for a meeting to discuss the latest deadline, missed meetings drain your precious time and are not productive. Always send an email or a text message (if you typically text the contact) to confirm the meeting and remind the other person about the agenda (if there is one).

Learn When to Say No

There's no doubt—bosses prefer employees who say "yes." So do friends, relatives, and acquaintances. You won't win many fans if you always say "no," but it's helpful to consider how you can find a balance between maintaining your indispensable status at work and your sanity. Unfortunately, there are no easy answers. Everyone's circumstances are different, and if you work in a place where you're only as good as the last thing you've done, not all of this advice may work for you. However, in many cases, once you've created a reputation for being helpful and agreeable, carefully choosing times to say "no" may not hurt your reputation at work; you may actually earn additional respect.

If it's a stressful time, you're up for a promotion, and the boss comes to you with a desperate request for help on a deadline, it's not the time say "no." On the other hand, if the situation isn't overly tense and there are other people who could help out, it may be a good opportunity to politely say it.

Say No without Saying No

Perhaps you've been carefully tracking your work and projects, but your boss forgot about the many items you're juggling right now. Instead of saying, "No, I cannot take on one more project," say, "I can see how important this project is. Can we sit down for a few minutes so you can help me prioritize my work? I want to be sure to focus on the most important things." Bring your itemized list of work and organized deadline notes to the meeting. Don't forget to include your day-to-day work in addition to any special projects you're managing. If you can make a solid case indicating that you really don't have time to handle another thing, it's possible you can say "no" without actually uttering that word.

Another great way to say "no" without seeming unhelpful is to suggest an alternate solution. Perhaps you are too busy to take on the work by yourself, but you can handle one part of the project. If you have a specialty area (for example, you're the best at planning and organizing strategy at the outset), suggest that you could manage that piece of the project and partner with someone who specializes in the next item on the to do list.

Without a doubt, this is a tricky conversation, as you are trying to deflect pieces of a project away from you. However, if you maintain an enthusiastic, "can do" approach and communicate effectively with your boss, it's possible you can trick him or her into thinking you're still saying "yes," even though you are really saying "no."

How to Give a Firm No

What qualifies as a good reason to say no at work will vary from office to office. Some people work in places where "no" is never an acceptable response. In these cases, it's best to deflect parts of the project when possible and to ask your supervisor to help restructure your priorities. However, sometimes you may need to turn down work due to other obligations. Keep in mind: if you take on a project and cannot meet the deadline, people will consider you unreliable.

If you already have planned time off to attend a family wedding or your child's graduation and this new project will interfere with that, you may choose to tell your boss that you cannot help. Ideally, you won't lead the conversation with the word "no." Instead, choose your words carefully and remind your supervisor that you always like to say "yes," but the circumstances prevent you from taking on this work. Then do your best to be helpful in passing along the project to someone else.

In Summary: Action Tips

You can plan ahead for your future. Follow the suggestions in this chapter. Here's a review of effective action items:

- Identify necessary steps and create a vision board to help you visualize them.

- Write down steps to get from where you are today to where you want to be.
- Leverage a mind map to help you accomplish those steps.
- Fit your short-term goals around the long-term goals and identify how they work together.
- Don't forget about how important it is to track deadlines. Be flexible, get a handle on your schedule (be sure to confirm meetings so you don't waste your time), and ask for help if you need it.
- Learn to say "no" without actually saying no, and always be prepared to back up and prove what you need when you're expressing your own concerns.

9 Prioritizing for Productivity

When you manage your time and your life effectively, deadlines are key. Understanding and setting priorities will help guide you daily to accomplish those deadlines. Once you set priorities, you'll have guideposts and road maps to ensure you accomplish your tasks.

How to Set Priorities

One of Dictionary.com's definitions of *priorities* is "something given special attention." The trick to defining your priorities is to decide which of the many items on your to-do lists require special attention, and then to rank those items.

Is it as easy as one, two, three? Perhaps not. Complicating factors when setting priorities may include:

- Competing work and personal priorities
- Multiple supervisors with different goals

- Unclear or changing deadlines
- Complexity of the task
- Scarcity of resources
- Availability of time

With so many factors affecting how you set priorities, it would be easy to fall into the trap of creating an overly complicated system (for example, a flow chart to rank each priority). However, since you likely haven't added an item on your to-do list dedicated to ranking complex priorities, the best approach is to simplify and quickly break down your list into several categories. For example:

Must-Do Items

If you don't accomplish these tasks, there will be big consequences. Sometimes, these are personal items—such as attending important family functions or events. More often, these are work related tasks you need to address in order to keep your job. If "heads will roll" if you failed to do something, categorize it here.

Daily Tasks

This list includes everything you do to get through your day or week. These can be mundane tasks you handle at work or at home. You need to get these done, but the world won't end if you fail to do something on this list one time or if you're running a little late. For example, if you'd like to stop at the grocery store to pick up something you need later this week, but you don't absolutely need it tonight, categorize it here.

Nice-to-Dos

This list includes everything you'd like to do, if only you could find the time to fit them in. For example, join a book club, or read the latest novel by your favorite author. In some cases, certain work items may fall in this category. If you've been waiting for the right time to join a committee at work, for example, you may add it in this section of your priority categories.

Exercise: Create Your Priorities List

Use your to-do list and categorize everything into one of these three categories. Admittedly, some workplaces seem to assign a high priority to everything, so it may be challenging to parse out the truly "do or die" tasks from the mundane, daily work.

If you're having trouble differentiating between the categories, check in with your supervisor.

Consider color-coding your list to highlight work and personal priorities. It wouldn't be surprising if most of the high-priority items are work related, but be sure your nice-to-do list includes several items you want to address as soon as you have time. For example, if you want to research a degree program, or take a class to learn a new skill, include those when you categorize your priorities.

Use Time Pockets

How much time do you waste every day? For some, especially those who commute long distances or spend a lot of time waiting in lines or on telephone holds, it's an excessive amount of time. Can you be more productive in these down times? When you re-think how you use *time pockets*, or periods of time when you could be accomplishing something, it's easy to be more productive and to accomplish your priorities.

This strategy may require a bit of planning and a mindset shift. First, you'll want to outline your down time. This doesn't need to be a complex endeavor. If you commute via train and don't accom-plish anything on your checklist during that time, consider your entire commute to be a time pocket. Map out all the time you typi-cally spend in a day—between tasks or doing something (such as waiting in line)—when you could be getting something else done.

If you find you have many time pockets free, plan ahead for ways to use them. Are there articles you'd like to read, either in magazines or via your phone? Incorporate tools such as Feedly, or the aptly named app Pocket, to help you track information you'd like to review online. Or, keep a stack of magazines or other printed material handy so you can easily grab it on your way to somewhere you'll be in line. Are there books you've always wanted to read, but never had a chance? Access books on tape to listen to the next time you're exercising or have down time. Do you wish you could be more in touch with popular culture, sports, or gar-dening trends? Find a podcast and subscribe—this is a great way to use time pockets when you're driving or exercising. You'll always have something interesting to listen to, and you'll have a chance to learn something new instead of just sitting around. Use an app such as iTunes or Stitcher to find podcasts you'll enjoy.

Another strategy is to keep lists of quick items you can do while you're out and about. Even something as mundane as scheduling a doctor's appointment may sit on your to-do list for days or weeks if you're distracted or busy. If you keep a detailed list of these items, along with necessary information to make it easy to accomplish each task (such as a phone number), you can handle these punch out tasks easily and make your time productive.

Exercise: What kinds of items can you add to a time pocket to-do list? Take a few minutes to include some ideas. Don't forget to plan ahead so you'll have all the information you'll need to address the punch out list you create, such as phone numbers, names, deadlines, and other dates.

_____

_____

_____

_____

_____

_____

_____

_____

_____

_____

_____

_____

_____

_____

Tips to Master Productivity

Once you know how to sort your priorities, you're ready to learn how to be more productive. If you could get more done in less time, think about the items on your to-do list you could check off!

Set Goals and Make Lists

If you've followed the tips in Chapter 7, you already have useful, detailed lists. Chapter 8 outlines how to set long-term and short-term goals and milestones, so you are halfway to mastering productivity already! If you skipped those chapters, go back and review the advice, and complete the exercises.

It's easiest to address daily goals first to improve productivity. Review your to-do list and the amount of time assigned to accomplish each task. Then, consider incorporating a productivity tool like time boxing, the 80/20 rule, or the Pomodoro Method.

Time Boxing

The time boxing strategy says you should allocate a certain amount of time to an activity or project, and then finish it in that time. In other words, even if the deadline is three weeks away, if you time box the task for four hours, you should finish it in the four hours and be done instead of dragging the task out over the next few weeks. You can also time box a bigger project. For example, if it will take 12 hours to finish a project, you may want to box it into smaller, manageable pieces and get as much as you can done in each work session. This approach can help keep you from being overwhelmed by a large task, as well as ensure you accomplish your goals in a designated time.

You can easily use this technique for professional and personal tasks. For example, if you have a big pile of laundry, decide that you'll spend one hour getting it in the wash, folded, and put away. Select as much laundry as you can reasonably manage in the one hour for the day, and get that done.

For professional tasks, you can use time boxing to finish up small, dangling items on your to-do list. For example, if you've been meaning to reach a particular person to ask for information but you haven't been able to get in touch, you can time box 15 or 20 minutes to make a few calls or to identify someone else who can provide the information. Time boxing helps you avoid perfectionist tendencies. (You won't be tempted to look over those presentation slides for the hundredth time if you practice time boxing.) If you're typically a procrastinator, time boxing pushes you to get at least some parts of larger projects finished in a designated time frame.

Exercise: Build a Time Box

J.D. Meier provides useful suggestions about how to get started using time boxing on his blog.* He suggests identifying items to time box, clarifying your objectives, setting an appropriate amount of time to finish the work, and completing the work in the time frame. Finally, you should evaluate the process and adapt it for the next time, if necessary.

You won't know if this is a good productivity technique for you until you try it. Follow the steps outlined as follows to create a time box. Start out with a small project. Meier suggests identifying an area where you lose a lot of time and selecting a project in that realm to box. Make sure you understand your objectives for the selected project. Don't try to time box anything unless you understand the scope of the project and your deadline. Use that

---

*J.D. Meier's Blog; http://blogs.msdn.com/b/jmeier/archive/2007/10/21/how-to-use-time-boxing-for-getting-results.aspx

information to decide how much time you should spend on the work, and follow the timeframe. Spend the allotted time wisely; don't count time when you're distracted, checking emails or your phone, or being interrupted. Once you finish, you'll be able to assess how well you did. If you underestimated the amount of time it would take, be sure you're honest about why the project took longer than expected. Could you have finished in the allotted time if you tried harder? Were your objectives incorrect, and that is why you couldn't finish in time? What could you do differently to make time boxing work for you?

Step 1: Identify items to time box.

_____

_____

_____

_____

_____

_____

_____

_____

Step 2: Clarify your objectives.

_____

_____

_____

_____

_____

_____

_____

_____

_____

_____

Step 3: Determine the appropriate amount of time.

_____

_____

_____

_____

_____

_____

_____

_____

Step 4: Work within your time box. (You can mark off the dates you time boxed here.)

_____

_____

_____

_____

_____

_____

_____

_____

_____

Step 5: Evaluate and adapt. (What did you finish or not finish. Do you need to have more time for something?)

_____

_____

_____

_____

_____

_____

_____

_____

_____

_____

_____

Use the 80/20 Rule

This rule, also known as the Pareto principle (named after the Italian economist Vilfredo Pareto), suggests 80% of outcomes result

Sometimes, it's helpful to give yourself an incentive to be productive. What motivates you to get things done? Is it the promise of a spa day after a big project is over? Maybe your incentive can be time to catch up on your favorite television show if you accomplish a particular goal in a set time? Use whatever motivates you to help accomplish the levels of productivity you want to reach.

from 20% of efforts. For example, many in the business world say 80% of sales come from 20% of clients. When applying this rule to productivity, it requires you to ask yourself if 80% of your outcomes result from 20% of your efforts. If so, you must focus on the 20% of work or projects you need to complete before you work on the bottom 80%.

Chalene Johnson, motivational speaker, author, and fitness celebrity, shared insights on her blog about how to leverage this rule to help improve your productivity. She suggests identifying a push goal, which is the goal that will have the most impact on you. Review your vision board and consider your long- and short-term goals. Ask yourself, "Which of these goals will make the biggest difference for me if I accomplish it?" If you work on that goal, you'll put the 80/20 rule to work.

Johnson suggests these ways to accomplish more via the 80/20 rule:

- Choose the top 20% of things on your list and focus on those before anything else.
- Ask yourself, "What is the most important thing I should do right now?" Then, do that one thing and do not be distracted.
- Don't try to do everything at one time. Focus on what is most important.

Exercise: Select Your Top 20%

Review your short- and long-term to-do lists. Select the top 20%, the most important items. Keep those highlighted and featured on your running lists and make a point to address items necessary to complete those items every day.

Use the Pomodoro Technique®

The Pomodoro Technique (http://pomodorotechnique.com) is a popular productivity approach with the goal of training your brain to focus on one task and to avoid distractions. According to the website dedicated to the technique, it is useful to help people use time well, eliminate burnout, overcome distractions, and achieve a strong work-life balance. The site explains that this technique helps people:

- Identify how much effort (in time) a task requires
- Protect themselves from interruptions and distractions when working on a task
- Accurately estimate the time it takes to accomplish tasks
- Use time well
- Set a timetable based on the work that needs to get done
- Organize their work and create more free time
- Improve the quality and efficiency of their output

To incorporate this technique into your productivity plan, follow these instructions:

- Eliminate all distractions. This includes digital and computer distractions such as email, texts, and social media, as well as phone calls and in-person interruptions. If you have a door for your office, using this technique may require you to close it, or to post a sign requesting no interruptions.
- Choose a project or task to focus on.

- Set a timer for 25 minutes.
- Work consistently and diligently on the task until the timer rings.
- Take a five-minute break.
- After four pomodoros (the name for each 25-minute session), take a longer break of 15 or 20 minutes.

Since many people fail to be productive due to interruptions and distractions, the 25-minute sprints to accomplish as much as possible before taking a break helps prevent this non-productive work time. Using this prescription, in 2.25 hours, you'd work 100 minutes and use 35 minutes as breaks. While it may seem like a lot of designated down time, consider how many minutes you truly work in any two- or three-hour period.

Sean Kennedy, a freelance MailChimp expert and marketer, suggested several time tracking apps on the Zapier blog (https://zapier.com/blog/best-time-tracking-apps/) that work on different platforms, including Web, iOS, or Android. Consider a free trial to help you determine how much time you spend working (or not working):

- Toggl
- Hours
- Everhour
- Paydirt
- Timely

Alternatively, you can use less high-tech tools to track your time, such as paper and pen or an Excel spreadsheet listing start and stop times. The main goal is to determine how much time you spend working and how much time you may waste.

Expect What You Can't Plan

No matter how well you adhere to the best productivity tips, the unexpected will happen. However, if you're always expecting the unexpected, it will be easy to adjust as necessary. Keep the following tips in mind.

Set Aside Time to Take Care of Anything Unexpected

When you plan your time and create your lists, always incorporate buffers for the unexpected. Simultaneously, make a habit of getting ahead of your list when you can—you'll be glad you did when an emergency comes up and prevents you from following your normal routine, even if only for a day.

Some Things Take a Little Longer Than Anticipated

If you track your time regularly, you'll have a good idea of how long it takes to do most things. However, there are always times when a project throws you for a loop and takes longer than you thought it would. Don't let this frustrate you. Take it in stride and flexibly adapt to the situation.

Leave Time for Errors

Mistakes happen. Whether the mistake is your fault, or someone else is responsible, the result is the same: your carefully planned schedule can be thrown off kilter. The goal of planning and being mindful of time and productivity is to help you take this all in stride. Don't be frustrated when things don't go as planned—use it as a learning opportunity to help you plan for and handle the future.

Create a Productive Mindset

There's more to being productive than making lists and using time-tracking apps. In many cases, your mindset affects productivity as much as your planning. For example, if you don't get enough sleep or agree to prioritize important items, such as your personal well-being, all of the apps and planning in the world may not help. Commit to giving yourself permission to have downtime, even during your busiest, most stressful periods. Research suggests that we aren't wired to work 24/7, despite what society may suggest (or what your boss may expect). The good news is, if you follow the tips in this chapter and the rest of the book, you'll be prepared to take advantage of every minute of your day, and to decide how you'll use each minute effectively. Whether you choose to daydream with your time pocket or catch up on some reading, it's up to you!

In Summary: Action Tips

Well-set priorities will help ensure you accomplish your goals. Take these steps to help you achieve your deadlines.

- Separate your must-do from want-to-do items and create your priorities list.
- Set goals and make action lists. Decide what motivates you to get work done.
- Try techniques such as time boxing, the 80/20 rule, time pockets, and the Pomodoro Method to get your work done.
- Expect the unexpected—and plan for it.
- Create a productive mindset by working during your most productive hours and taking breaks.

10 Organizing Your Work Environment

All the planning, list making, and vision boarding in the world won't make a difference to you if your work environment isn't set up to help you accomplish your goals. Even if you aren't typically well organized, you can still take certain steps to help ensure you can get everything done in an orderly, systemized way. Here's a bonus: If you appear organized, you won't attract negative attention or have colleagues questioning your professionalism behind your back as a result of your untidy workspace.

Is a Clean Desk Preferable?

Is a messy desk the sign of a cluttered mind or a brilliant mind? Researchers investigated how a messy work environment affects people. In their paper, "Physical Orderliness Changes Decisions and Behaviors," Kathleen D. Vohs, Joseph P. Redden, and Ryan

Rahinel of the University of Minnesota (http://behaviorlab.org/Papers/Messy.pdf) found that working in an orderly environment led participants to make healthier food choices and to be more generous financially. Researchers interpreted the findings to suggest that sitting in a tidy room led people to choose "desirable, normatively-good" behaviors.

However, they also determined that disorder (a messy desk) does appear to result in more creativity. Their hypothesis, "Sitting in a messy, disorderly room would stimulate more creative ideas than sitting in a tidy, orderly room" was shown to be true in their experiment. They suggest that "disorderly laboratory stimulated creativity because it violated participants' expectations, which past work has shown can aid creativity."

Whether or not a messy desk really helps inspire creativity, you risk alienating those who don't feel productive in a messy environment—especially if you work in an open space or co-workers either pass by or need to work with you around your untidy space. In other words, while you may not believe your messy workspace negatively affects you, it could be interfering with your co-workers' ability to get their work done without being distracted.

Another study, conducted by researchers from Rice University, Pennsylvania State University, and Arizona State University, indicated that subjects exposed to what they considered "disgusting" situations had a tendency to remove themselves from the situation and to focus on themselves more than other people. In an article for NineMSN,* contributing author Vikas Mittal said, "If there is less likelihood to feel disgusted, there will be a lower likelihood that people need to be self-focused and there will be a higher likelihood for people to cooperate with each other." Dr. Lisa A Williams, from the University of New South Wales's School of Psychology, added insights from related research that might give someone with a potentially disgusting workplace pause. She said, ". . . When we're

---

*http://coach.ninemsn.com.au/2015/02/16/16/45/a-clean-desk-could-make-you-a-better-person

feeling disgusted, we are more likely to judge the moral actions of others more harshly."

Whether your messy workspace makes you more creative or not, if the clutter, wrappers, and half-eaten lunches annoy or disgust your tidier colleagues, you could be putting your professional reputation in jeopardy. Messiness may set you up to be judged to a harsher standard than your colleagues, which could be challenging if you want a promotion.

How to Clean Up Your Workspace

Keeping an organized workspace can improve your reputation at work and make it a lot easier for you to find everything you need. Consider the time you can save if you don't need to dig through mounds of papers when you want to find something, or spend designated time to clean up your things.

Eliminate Paper

Most productivity experts advise that you eliminate every item you don't need to keep. Have you been printing out emails and saving them? Unless you have a specific mandate to do so, you should find a paper-free way to store those items. File the emails themselves in a folder in your email system, download them to a back-up, or scan and store digital copies. Shred and throw away the rest. Eliminate any piece of paper that could be tossed or stored electronically.

Focus on one area of your office at a time. Perhaps you'll go through one drawer per day and clean each of them out before you attack your desktop. Having usable storage space makes it a lot easier to organize your materials.

This tactic works for Michael Valente, a financial risk manager. He says, "Throw everything out. Eliminate hard copies unless you work with contracts and legal documents and only maintain electronic files. I put all paper in the recycle bin, and my desk has never been cleaner."

HOW TO GO PAPER-FREE

If you have excessive amounts of paperwork, approach the clean up task one step at a time. Either invest in a scanner or tap into some applications that work with your smartphone to digitize your paperwork. For example:

- **Evernote's Scannable app (iOS):** Save scans to Evernote or other apps to easily share them with colleagues via email or SMS.
- **Google Drive (Android and iOS):** Scan documents and perform optical character recognition on text in the materials you scan.
- **CamScanner (Android, iOS, and Windows):** Scans documents to PDF; can handle multiple page or batch scanning.

Exercise: Choose a Paper-Free App
Start with these suggested apps, Google ideas for paperless storage, or ask a friend for suggestions of apps to help you become paper-free in your office or home. Take some time to evaluate a few and try one out for at least a week.

Collect and Redistribute

Perhaps you can't eliminate *all* of the paper from your workspace. If that's the case, then the next best thing is to find a place for everything and put it there. Collect everything (paper, supplies, decorations, etc.) and redistribute each to its proper home. If you have a lot of papers to save, file them neatly and label them clearly so they will be easily accessible when you need them.

While you're collecting, decide what really needs to be on your desk. Do you really need three staplers, two rechargers, eight sticky pads of paper, and five framed family photos? Pare everything down. The less you keep on your desk in your prime working real estate, the more organized you will appear.

Another piece of useful advice for offices: be sure your trash can reasonably accommodates your garbage. If you have a tiny trash bin and you can't even fit the leftover plate from your lunch in it, you're more likely to keep gross garbage that you should have immediately thrown out. If your work trash receptacle isn't big enough, get another one. You'll save yourself a lot of time and aggravation in the long run.

KEEP IMPORTANT ITEMS IN SIGHT

Are you someone who subscribes to the adage, "Out of sight, out of mind"? If so, be sure to address your need to see what you need to do when you're organizing your office. If filing important papers by date or topic may result in you forgetting to take care of them, consider hanging a bulletin board or white board. Mark off the board with important deadlines so you won't miss anything. The advantage of a bulletin board is that you can pin important notes directly to the board to remind yourself, but a white board with written reminders may be less likely to get cluttered. Choose carefully—you don't want to risk pinning so many items to a bulletin board that you wind up with a new messy surface to keep clean.

Be mindful of your habits, and choose the surface most likely to help you keep organized if you want to maintain sightlines with your deadlines and to-dos.

Mark Urgent and Non-Urgent Items

Just as your to-do list should be separated between urgent and non-urgent items, you should parse out those categories when you organize. This includes organizing your papers (if you keep papers), as well as your computer desktop into high-use and low-use sections.

Plan Your Space

One of the cardinal rules of organizing is to put something in close proximity to where you use it. If you frequently jot things down on a pad of paper, keep the paper and pens in an easily accessible drawer or on top of your desk. If you're a fan of sticky notes, make sure they are always in reach. If possible, keep all of your supplies in one organized drawer.

Create a designated place to keep papers or other materials you'll need on any given day. If you prepared a file to bring to a meeting tomorrow, make sure you'll know exactly where to find it when you arrive in the morning. If you successfully arrange everything, and everything has its right place, you'll save time every day you would have otherwise spent looking for items or coming in early in case you needed to recreate materials for meetings.

Don't Be Afraid to Discard

No matter how you try to avoid paper, most people inevitably receive a lot of unnecessary junk, along with potentially more valuable information that you don't want to lose. Consider creating two inboxes. One will be for materials you've already reviewed and need to file or sort and the other will be for items you have not reviewed yet. The famous circular file/trash can is the best spot for anything you identify as useless. The secret is to *not keep* things you know you'll never review or items you don't need. If it's not important to you, eliminate it forever and do not clutter your workspace. You may decide that the rest of the paperwork you receive should be digitized, given or thrown away, or properly filed and off your desk.

Whether you create an inbox, bin, or a special file in a cabinet for information you need to address at a later time, make sure you don't put anything away so well that you'll never see it again. If you have a revolving series of important paperwork coming into your office, create a calendar-oriented group of files. For example, you may put everything in a file labeled "for the month," so you know when you need to address it. Or, digitize the documents, organize them accordingly, and add them to your online calendar.

Sharlyn Lauby, author of the workplace blog HR Bartender, explains the system that works for her:

> *I file paper in accordion folders by month or day. If I'm going to a meeting on the 30th, I put it in the tab labeled 29th so I review the information the day before the meeting. Or, if I want to budget for a conference next year, I put it in the tab for the month that I do budgeting. At the beginning of each month, I organize my papers by day. This system keeps paper—and distractions—off my desk. The only things on my desk are the things I'm working on.*

Exercise: Declutter Your Space

Choose a realistic space to declutter. It can be at work or at home. Follow the advice in this chapter to eliminate extra items you don't need, and to store materials you rely on regularly in a place where you can find them. Do this for 20 minutes a day until the space is cleaned up.

Add Expiration Dates

If you do keep paper and file them daily or weekly, be sure you make a habit of throwing away outdated versions of materials you're saving or items you no longer need. Add expiration dates to some of your files. Whether or not you file items by date, add a note or include some designation in your file if the materials expire. For example, color code the folders or file tabs if the material is time-sensitive and does not require saving forever.

Keep Your Computer Desktop Organized

Even if you eliminate all the paper in your office, you may still have a disorganized mess on your computer's desktop. Even if you're the only one who uses your computer, and the trash there may not interfere with anyone else's peaceful work environment, you don't want to keep a slew of files you can never find. Just as you shouldn't leave stacks of disorganized paper on your actual desk, don't leave virtual piles on your computer. Keep current items in folders on your desktop, in addition to shortcuts to programs you use on a regular basis. Don't forget to empty your computer's trash, since it saves valuable memory and clears out items you no longer need.

Create Labeled Folders

At work and on your personal computer, you'll want to create folders to capture your most important information. At work, that may include written directives or instructions from your boss or clients. At home, perhaps it's photos or files with menus or recipes from parties you've planned and want to refer to again. Determine what you want to save, and immediately file it in the appropriate folder so you'll be able to find it when you need it. Then, determine what you don't need and discard right away. Your computer will be as neat as your actual desktop.

Get Organized at Home

Once you become an expert in organization strategies at work, you can use the same tactics at home. You likely accumulate a lot of junk mail, bills, fliers, and magazines. If you have children, school paperwork alone may overwhelm a designated inbox. It's easy to lose an important bill or permission slip if you don't immediately sort and organize materials as they come into your house. If you can't keep up with everything, it costs you time (finding things you need) and money (if you fail to pay a bill).

If you don't live alone, one difference in your at-home organizational system is you'll need to convince everyone else to buy into the system. Otherwise, you could be facing an uphill battle of trying to file or toss materials while your family members or roommates actively work against your newly implemented plan. Try to make things as easy as possible for everyone to implement.

Cynthia Ewer, author of *The Complete Idiot's Guide to Getting Organized*, suggests organizing your home filing system into several categories:

Action File

Ewer suggests using a tabletop file to keep things such as bills and other information that requires immediate attention or replies. This to-do file makes it easy to access information you need to handle right away, and ensures nothing is out of sight.

Basic Files

Keep paperwork you need for the long term in a labeled file drawer where you store important documents you may need to reference. Ewer suggests this might include "medical insurance records, credit card statements, rent receipts, and bank statements." Put these files somewhere you can easily access when you're working on paying your bills, doing your taxes, assessing your medical records, or reviewing home maintenance records.

Classic Files

This is where Ewer says you should maintain your long-term file archives: "Copies of tax returns and insurance policies, homeowners' records, medical records, and copies of legal documents belong in classic files." She explains that you should keep original legal documents and items such as insurance policies or tax records in a safe box. You may also want to consider digitizing these items to store for safekeeping.

Regardless of how you organize your paperwork, try to select a convenient location to file your items. Otherwise, it's unlikely you'll ever put everything away!

Start with a Clean Sink

Even if you live alone, it's easy for things to get disorganized. Fly-Lady.net, a site dedicated to help control clutter and chaos, bit-by-bit, attests you can help stave off a messy home by always making sure your kitchen sink is clean of dishes and shiny. What does a messy house have to do with the sink? FlyLady's hypothesis is that every baby step you take to help keep yourself organized affects everything else. If you have a clean sink, she suggests, you'll be less likely to allow items to clutter the rest of your kitchen or to over-flow into the rest of the house.

Don't Let Everything Build Up

Look around your home and identify places where you (or other household members) tend to drop things. What are the messy areas? What areas may look messy, and may contribute to a mindset that encourages a messy house? For example, if shoes pile up near the door, a quick fix could be a shoe rack or a bin for shoes. If the area near the door doesn't look cluttered, people may be discouraged from dumping other items in that location. Taking one small step to cut clutter could have a ripple affect if you can stave off other messes that would naturally collect around your entranceway.

If a particular piece of furniture becomes a catch-all for junk you don't need, incorporate mechanisms to keep the area from getting cluttered. For example, put a basket to capture items and make a point to move, file, or toss things instead of allowing them to build up and look messy.

Ultimately, if you can prevent messes from racking up, you'll save time later. Consider how long it takes to file and put away a month's worth of materials, not to mention possibly finding things you needed, but never found when you wanted them? If you take into account the possible late charges from unpaid and misplaced bills or the social cost of lost invitations from friends who did not receive your RSVP, the few minutes a day spent tidying up those high-risk areas in your home can be very valuable.

Try to make a habit of "one touch organizing." In other words, instead of flipping through the mail and planning to sort it later, put everything in its place at the first touch. Don't look at the mail, for example, unless you are prepared to sort it! Stand near the garbage and your designated bins, and touch everything one time to sort it. You'll save time and avoid collecting unsightly clutter.

Practice Mindful Buying and Giving Away

You likely already know if you own too many things. Are your bookcases cluttered with items you don't have time to dust? Is your closet bursting at the seams with things you haven't worn in years? Do you always shop ahead for gifts, but you can never find them when it's time to do the gifting? If you answered "yes" to any of these questions, it's likely time for an intervention to help you get more organized and less overwhelmed.

Organizers advise you to give two items away for every one thing you bring into your house. If you're committed to a less complicated, more organized lifestyle, consider what you can eliminate from your home before you bring in something new. Typically, it's easiest to do this for clothing. What haven't you worn in a year or two? Remove those items from your wardrobe and donate them to someone who may be able to use them. Don't stop with your closet, though. Consider finding a new place for anything that's taking up space in your home that you don't need. If you haven't gone through your possessions in some time, you may be surprised by how many things you can give away or throw away. Review and purge at least twice a year. Otherwise, you risk becoming so overwhelmed by extra stuff that you'll never have time to clean and organize your life!

In Summary: Action Tips

When you organize your work environment, you'll benefit in many ways. In addition to saving time finding items, you'll make a stronger impression on colleagues and potentially improve your reputation at work.

- Clean up your work space. Eliminate clutter, extra paper, and things you don't need.
- Set up procedures and places to sort your paperwork, and mark things urgent or not urgent.
- Find a place to collect items before you file them, and mark dates on materials so you know when to deal with them.
- Organize your computer's desktop so you can be more efficient.
- Get organized at home, too. Find places to keep materials you need to store and file. Clean your sink. Don't let clutter build up at home. Give away something every time you bring something new into your home.

11 Presenting Your Best Self at Meetings

When you're getting organized at work, be sure to consider how to put your best foot forward at meetings, especially if it's likely that attending meetings will be part of your weekly or daily routine. Learn to make the most of this time. Do not waste these opportunities to introduce yourself to new people and solidify good impressions. When you manage your time at meetings well, you can use them to your advantage and reduce the feeling that they are just a necessary evil.

You've likely heard that people form an impression of you in the first few seconds after you meet. Meetings, aptly named, are important opportunities to make good impressions on people you work with or people with whom you'd like to do business. Take advantage of the opportunity to put your best foot forward, to make a strong first impression during meetings.

Dress for Success

Make sure you know the dress code for the meeting before you attend. Is it a casual get together, or will people be a little more dressed up? Conventional wisdom suggests you should dress for the job you want, not the job you have. Similarly, it's not a bad idea to dress a step above what might be expected if you want to make a good impression. However, if everyone will be wearing jeans and t-shirts, don't show up in a suit. Consider wearing a signature item, such as a unique tie (if it's a dressy affair), a scarf, or a piece of jewelry. Doing so can help you become more memorable when you get in touch with people after the meeting. For example, you may say, "I was the one in the pink tie."

Plan ahead (the night before!) so you're prepared to wear an outfit you choose instead of whatever is available. You don't want to rush around the morning of an important meeting trying to find something clean and pressed to wear.

Arrive on Time and
Ready to Start the Meeting

Even if you're not in charge and your tardiness will not delay the meeting, you should always be on time or early. Perhaps meetings you attend don't usually start on time. Even if most people wander in late, make a point to arrive on time, even if you know you'll be the only one who is punctual.

When you're late, it's disrespectful to the people in the meeting who may need to fill you in on what you missed. Everyone is busy and has many priorities; you are not the only one with a long to-do list. If you are always late, people will assume your inability to arrive on time implies you aren't attentive to details (at best), or you aren't trustworthy (at worst). Tardiness implies you don't value other people's time. You implicitly suggest your time is more important than their time. On the flip side, simply arriving early for a scheduled appointment suggests you appreciate and value your colleagues. When you are responsible about time, your colleagues (and friends) will trust you and assume you're organized and dependable.

Don't ruin your on-time arrival by making a mad dash to the meeting with your important papers trailing behind you, only to anxiously ask your seatmate to borrow a pen. Just getting to the meeting is a good first step, but you lose all the credibility assigned to someone who arrives on time if you are physically in attendance but mentally unprepared to meet. Collect your materials and your thoughts before you arrive.

Tips to Make Sure You're on Time—Every Time

Reduce your stress levels and guarantee you will be on time by preparing in advance. Use the following tips to help you stay on track.

Spread Out Your Appointments

If you're meeting with your long-winded boss or colleague, don't plan a meeting immediately following—especially in a different office or location. Expect the unexpected and leave yourself plenty of time to travel between meetings, even if it's just one floor away. Schedule meetings at reasonable intervals to account for other people being late, a meeting not starting on time, or an appointment unexpectedly running longer than usual. Give yourself time to finish one appointment and regroup, and collect your materials before the next one.

Consider Travel Time

If possible, don't schedule appointments that put you smack in the middle of rush hour to get where you need to go. If you have a choice, find off-peak times to travel to meet people, when you're less likely to encounter unexpected delays.

Run Through a Mental Checklist

Some things on this checklist are obvious, such as "collect your paperwork." Other items are easier to forget. For example, if you're driving to a meeting first thing in the morning, do you have enough gas in your car to get there? If you're perpetually late, don't assume you'll get up early the next day with enough time to stop for gas. Prepare in advance and you'll avoid unexpected surprises that result in you being late. Are you useless without your morning cup of coffee? Plan time to fill your cup. Are you in charge of bringing snacks? Get them in advance. The fewer items you need to check off your list right before a meeting, the better.

Plan to Arrive Early

If you mentally add in a 10- or 15-minute buffer, you'll rarely be late for meetings.

Don't Try to Cram Another Item into Your To-Do List

While you do want to use as much of your time as possible productively, when you have a few minutes to spare before a meeting, don't check your email or respond to important text messages in an effort to make the most of every second. Inevitably, you'll encounter something that drains more of your time than the few minutes you have. Or, you'll be faced with a new problem that may distract you from being your best self in your meeting that is only minutes away. While you want to use all of your time well, don't do so to the point of depriving yourself of crucial time to prepare and get yourself ready for the meeting at hand.

Stop What You're Doing and Go

Keep your priorities straight. When it's time to go to the meeting, collect your things and go. You'll arrive prepared, unstressed, and free from distractions.

REMEMBER NAMES

When you attend meetings with people you're just meeting for the first time, don't miss the opportunity to learn their names. Too often, people are distracted or don't pay attention during introductions and realize later they never caught the person's name. Don't let that happen to you. As you meet each new person, repeat his or her name. Instead of, "It's so nice to meet you," say, "Veronica, it's a pleasure to meet you." If, for some reason, you missed the person's name, ask for it again and then repeat it. "Miranda, that was my preschool best friend's name." Try to repeat the person's name at the beginning, middle, and end of your conversation or introduction. People like to hear their own names, so you'll win points for saying it over again.

Try to think of a way to remember your new contact's name. You may think to yourself, "Daniel, like my brother." Or, "April, like April Showers." BuildYourMemory.com suggests: "In order to remember that the name of a tall, thin man that you have just been introduced to is Mr. Adamson, you might try visualizing the biblical first man 'Adam' (complete with fig leaf), holding a little boy in his arms. Adam's son—Adamson." Another suggestion is to make an association with the name. For example, "Tall Tim" or "Handsome Harry."

Identify a Goal

If you want to make a strong first impression, identify your goal going into the meeting. Know what you want to get from the interaction. Perhaps you need to clarify details about an assignment. Or, you want to convince someone you can take on additional responsibility. If you know what you want to accomplish during the meeting, it's much easier to reach your goals or, alternatively, to evaluate and assess reasons why you may not have successfully accomplished what you set out to do. Be mindful and hold yourself accountable for each meeting and you'll have more successes to count down the road.

Be Positive

If you've ever been in a meeting where a participant actively shot down everything anyone said and spent the entire meeting shaking his head disapprovingly, you've witnessed how *not* to act in a meeting. While you don't need to be a "yes person" or cheerfully endorse everything other colleagues suggest in meetings, don't be pegged as the person who never likes anything or who has concerns with everything discussed. This is especially true if you're critical without offering suggestions to help address or solve issues. You will not make a favorable impression if you are excessively negative. Save your critiques for when they matter most and try to be a team player the rest of the time.

Body Language Matters

When you meet new people, do your best to visibly project your interest and enthusiasm. When you arrive at the meeting, make eye contact with other participants. Offer a pleasant smile and a firm handshake. For a proper business handshake, extend your right hand, look at the person's eyes, smile, and grip firmly, but do not give a death grip. Shake two or three times, then let go. Try to avoid shaking hands with sweaty palms. If you tend to have clammy hands, keep a handkerchief or small cloth to wipe your hands. Avoid a limp or weak handshake, as people will think you're not capable if you can't shake hands in a confident manner. However, there's no need to crush the other person's hand. Grip firmly, but not as if you are trying to squeeze the life out of the other person.

Don't underestimate the importance of the smile when you meet. If you grimace, appear distracted, or otherwise suggest you're less than interested in meeting the other person, your reputation may forever be marred. Smile with your eyes and your mouth, and people will be more likely to remember you with a positive feeling.

Maintain an open stance so you appear welcoming and interested in meeting people. Stand and sit up straight and don't slouch. Keep your stomach in, your shoulders back, and your head up. Consider where your chin is pointing. If it is facing your chest, you are probably slouching. Keep your chin tipped slightly up. Take your hands out of your pockets and avoid crossing your arms in front of you.

PUT AWAY YOUR PHONE

Dividing your attention by reviewing your phone in a meeting sends a clear signal you're not completely committed to what is happening in the room. At best, you'll miss something important, and at worst, everyone in the meeting will think you're rude and have no manners. Don't take this lightly. Academic research suggests viewing your phone during meetings is a bad idea. In their article for *Business Communication Quarterly*, Melvin Washington, Ephraim Okoro, and Peter Cardon noted that courtesy, including "manners, business etiquette, graciousness, and respectfulness," is a crucial workplace skill, even more key to hiring managers than other important employee characteristics, such as "responsibility, interpersonal skills, positive attitude, professionalism, work ethic and teamwork skills."

Their article outlines research showing that the majority of people surveyed believe using mobile devices during meetings is rude. It notes that 84% of those surveyed think it's inappropriate to write texts or emails during formal meetings, 75% believe it is inappropriate to read texts or emails during formal meetings, and 66% responded they think it's inappropriate to write texts or emails during any meetings. The study found that younger professionals are more accepting of mobile phone use during meetings, and women are far less accepting of mobile phone use during informal meetings.

Regardless of the age or gender of the people at your meetings, it's best to put away your phone during meetings and prevent someone from judging you as rude or inconsiderate.

Stay Alert

If you've ever run a meeting and looked around to see people nodding off, you know it's important to look alert and attentive if you want to make a good impression at meetings. It won't matter if you arrive on time and prepared to work if you fall asleep!

Follow these tips to help ensure you stay awake and engaged, so you can make the most of every meeting you attend.

- **Avoid scheduling meetings right after lunch.** It's a known fact that people tend to be drowsy after lunch. If possible, do not schedule meetings for times when you're most likely to want a nap.
- **Get your body moving.** While it's not appropriate to launch into a series of jumping jacks or thrust yourself into your favorite yoga moves during a meeting, you can take a brisk walk before you arrive. Take the stairs instead of the elevator on your way to the meeting if possible. A little exercise can help prevent you from dozing off and making a poor impression.
- **Schedule meetings on the move.** Some companies, including Google, encourage their employees to schedule meetings on the go. In other words, to discuss topics during a walk instead of while seated at a table. While it makes it difficult to take detailed notes, and may not be appropriate for all meetings, if you could conduct your meeting while standing or walking, suggest it. You may find you benefit more from the meeting than you might expect.
- **Don't get too comfortable.** If the meeting room has cushy chairs that would likely tempt you to give in to your need for some extra z's, don't sit in them. If you're a little uncomfortable, you're less likely to drift off to sleep.
- **Do some (subtle) stretches.** While you don't want to fidget during the whole meeting (as it may distract your colleagues), a few timely stretches may help keep you more alert and attentive. If necessary, stand up and take a break. You may want to suggest a stretch break if it's a long meeting.
- **Sit in the front.** An age-old technique to encourage people to pay attention, sitting in the front ensures you are visible to anyone who attends the meeting. Make eye contact with the meeting leader and you're less likely to nod off.

- **Take notes.** Even if some of your notes turn into doodles and drawings, actively participating in the meeting by taking notes helps you stay engaged. A side benefit of note taking is that you're more likely to remember important details if you write them down.
- **Participate.** Do you have ideas or suggestions? Raise your hand and share them. Actively involving yourself in the meeting is the best way to stay alert and ensure you don't disconnect and fall asleep.
- **Think about what you'd add.** Perhaps the meeting is so boring and has no redeeming features to encourage you to participate or stay awake. Challenge yourself to think of how you would run things differently. How would the agenda look? How much time would everyone have to speak? If the meeting's content isn't enough to hold your interest, try to find another reason to stay awake, even if it means quietly exercising your judgmental tendencies.
- **Drink water.** If you sip water throughout the meeting, it will help you stay alert. If it's appropriate for your meeting, consider snacking on something with protein during the meeting. Avoid sugar and carbohydrates, which can cause you to crash after eating them.

Follow Up

If you commit to following up after a meeting, make sure you do so. It's a good idea to send an email clarifying any specific details discussed, especially if they coordinate with action items for you. Even if there are no specific action items, send a brief note thanking the person/people in the meeting and mention future plans or opportunities to get in touch.

Exercise: Set Your Goal

It's easy to get wrapped up in the minutia of work and meetings. It's rare to take time to identify specific goals regarding something as common as a meeting. However, it is helpful to focus on these small things that take up your time everyday, as these are the building blocks of the bigger items you want to accomplish.

How can you improve your experiences in meetings? Use this chapter as a guide. Do you need a checklist of what to do before a meeting? Should you adjust your body language so you don't appear overly negative? Take the time now to set goals regarding your next meeting. How can you make a better impression? List your notes here.

_____

_____

_____

_____

_____

_____

_____

_____

_____

_____

_____

_____

_____

In Summary: Action Tips

If meetings are a part of your workday, make the most of these opportunities to shine using these tips.

- Make a good impression. Pay attention to what you wear and be on time.
- Decide on a goal and move purposefully to achieve it via the meetings you attend.
- Be positive, and watch your body language.
- Stay alert. Use the tips in this chapter to ensure you don't nod off during a meeting, no matter how boring it may be.
- Put away your phone.
- Always follow up.

12 Reviewing Your Progress Regularly

The most successful people in work and in life are mindful of what they hope to accomplish. They set goals, as described in Chapter 8, and regularly review their accomplishments to stay on track. Add accountability steps to your planning and monitor your goals so you can continue to move forward along the path you identified.

It's likely your workplace provides some checkpoints to help monitor your progress. Employers often mandate annual or bi-annual reviews. You may be required to conduct a self-assessment to help with the process. Participate fully in any review process your organization or employer offers and prepare to make the most of the opportunity to determine how far you've come in meeting your goals at work.

During your preparations, incorporate notes about how your role evolved in the organization. For example, did you take on new responsibilities? Are you supervising new people or reporting to someone new? When you assess the past six months or year, is there anything you need to explain?

Don't wait until the last minute to plan and evaluate. If you're highly motivated, you should institute self-checks throughout the year to keep yourself on track. Assuming you set specific goals, it will be easy to report your progress to your boss or to track it yourself.

Keep Records

Always track your own progress by making notes of accomplishments and wins at work. Be sure to document your successes, as discussed in Chapter 6, where we outlined steps to keep a brag record of accomplishments. Depending on your goals, your records may include anything from information about clients you helped land to files you organized to maintain an efficient office. Include details about how you helped colleagues with their wins, too. If you received thank you notes or accolades, save them for your records, and ask anyone willing to put a compliment in writing for you if they will add a recommendation to your LinkedIn profile.

If you're challenged to meet your goals, track that, too. Did you miss your target last quarter? Were there extenuating circumstances or specific reasons for the miss? Keep records to help you understand your progress (or lack of progress) at work. Be prepared to discuss your successes and to detail how you plan to overcome failures. Provide information about your plan. Keep notes and records to inform others, but also maintain details and information for yourself. What could you have done better or differently, in hindsight, to improve an outcome? What were the steps you took that led to a successful result? What should you duplicate next time to help ensure a similar result?

Use Your Checklists

Don't make lists and set them aside, only to review once or twice a year. Measure your progress regularly and note what items require more attention to allow you to check them off. If you're not checking through your designated items, determine what prevented you from accomplishing your goals and do what you can to adjust course. What needs to be in place to ensure you successfully achieve your plans? Do you need outside assistance or coaching or help managing your workload? Could you benefit from more accountability to ensure you meet your milestones? Track and rate your progress so you'll be able to effectively report on your accomplishments and move ahead with your goals.

In an article for *U.S. News & World Report*'s "On Careers" column, Chrissy Scivicque, CEO of "Eat Your Career," suggested asking yourself the following questions:

- What challenges have you overcome? How did you do it?
- What performance improvements have you made since your last review?
- Where do you still have room for improvement? How do you plan to address any issues preventing forward progress?
- What have you accomplished in the past year? (Be specific.)
- How have you contributed to the organization's bottom line?
- How have you increased your value to the organization over the past year?
- In what areas do you most excel? How can you continue to build on these strengths?
- How can you better use your skills for the good of the team and the organization?

If you're involved in a formal review process, you turn it into a "win-win" for you and your employer by delving into the reasons for your successes and failures. If you need support from your employer or organization to accomplish your goals to benefit both the company and you personally, make a case and ask for what you need. Your proposal should include benefits for the organization as a primary feature. For example, if your goal is to become certified in a skill you need to improve your performance at work, and you can document how the training would benefit your workplace, you'll have a good case to present your supervisor.

Prepare for Criticism

When you plan to be evaluated, prepare via the steps we've already covered. Prepare lists and documentation of your accomplishments, accolades, and successes. Explain how you plan to improve in areas where you were less successful than expected, and write down action points to discuss. This preparation is key, but also prepare mentally for (hopefully) constructive criticism and outside suggestions. It's one thing to create a list of what you plan to do better next time, it is another to internalize someone else's ideas about what you need to do differently in order to meet your goals and those of the organization.

If you have difficulty with criticism, plan to have an open mind. It's likely you aren't going to be blindsided by anything mentioned in a review, especially if you track your goals and accomplishments. If you already know where criticism may come, you'll be ready to internalize and leverage it to your advantage.

It's natural to feel intimidated by criticism—research shows that we're wired to view it as threatening. Instead of moving directly into defensive mode, try to understand your boss' concerns and ask questions to clarify anything you don't understand. Don't defend yourself, as you'll only appear difficult and not open to suggestions. Instead, ask for concrete examples. For example, if your supervisor says you're not attentive to details and you don't believe that's true, don't say, "I think I pay a lot of attention to details, and I have no idea what you're talking about." Instead, reply, "Can you give me an example of what you mean?"

Pay attention to your body language, too. More than 90% of communication is nonverbal. Even if you train yourself to say the "right" things, if you shake your head, clench your fists, grit your teeth, and fold your arms in front of you throughout the conversation (all signs you're feeling threatened and defensive), all your good intentions to appear open to criticism will be for nothing.

If you want to appear comfortable and confident, keep a relaxed posture and don't appear too stiff. Lean in slightly toward the other person to indicate you're really listening with intent. Allow your arms to relax at your sides instead of crossed in front of you and maintain eye contact. Even if your supervisor says something you don't like, don't break eye contact or look at the ground, as it suggests you're disengaging from that part of the conversation. Be particularly attentive to try to maintain the same relaxed and open body language throughout the conversation. It will be very obvious if you're open and smiling when you hear something you like, but closed with your arms crossed in front of you if you hear anything critical.

Ask for a follow-up appointment to go over any surprising feedback once you've had a chance to think about it and to identify any solutions you plan to suggest. Assume your supervisor has your best interests (and those of the organization) at heart and make the most of the advice, and be sure you understand it.

Exercise: Conduct Your Own Review

If you don't have a formal review with an employer (or, even if you do!), consider conducting your own evaluation. One way to assess how you're doing is to learn what other people think of you. A review that includes input from people in different parts of your life is a called a "360-degree review," so named because it aims to capture information from all around you (in a 360-degree circle). Since it's a little awkward to interview the people who work with you and to quiz them about what they think of you, there's an online resource to help accomplish the same goal.

Visit Reach Personal Branding's website (www.reachcc.com/360Reach) and sign up for a free, 15-day password to access their resources. The exercise requires you to connect with people you know to ask them to anonymously fill out a survey about you. You can use the results to assess how you're doing in terms of accomplishing your goals, especially if any of your plans involve influencing other people.

Identify Inefficiencies

Are you falling short with any of your goals? How can you be more efficient and accomplish more? Ideally, you'll check things off your short-term goals on a daily or weekly basis and make progress on those longer-term goals regularly, too. Don't wait for someone else to tell you how to make changes. If your to-do list needs more "do" and less "to," focus on how you can make it happen.

Review Your Goals

The first step is to review and evaluate your goals individually. Were you too optimistic when you set them? Have circumstances beyond your control interfered with getting things accomplished? One example of this might be someone in your family who has an emergency that requires your help. If you're using time you might have spent to fulfill your goals to address a family emergency, perhaps it's time to adjust your expectations regarding your goals a bit or to ask for help handling the emergency. Alternatively, you may find you didn't plan well or were overly optimistic about finishing certain items in a set period of time. For example, you knew you would be taking a class two evenings a week, but your goals also included joining some new committees at work. If you purposely set mutually exclusive goals, make a note to do better next time so you'll position yourself to reasonably move ahead with your plans and check things off of your list.

If you need to reevaluate and reset your goals, consider applying the "SMART" goal criteria, commonly attributed to Peter Drucker's management by objectives concept. Drexel.edu explains that SMART goals are:

- **Specific.** Indicate specific results and include examples. For example, "Exercise more" would become, "Visit the gym three times a week for 30 minutes each time."
- **Measurable.** Sometimes, it's easy to measure quantifiable results. Did you increase the number of clients to three from one? That's easily measured. Have you improved the efficiency of something? If it takes one hour to file work at the end of the day instead of two hours, that's a clear improvement. It's more difficult to measure changes in behavior or quality. For your own goals, note how you plan to measure them and how your employer will measure them.
- **Ambitious and achievable.** Are your goals challenging enough? If you easily accomplished everything, perhaps you need tougher goals or to push yourself a bit more.
- **Results-based.** What specific result do you expect? Will you be able to land a new job after earning a new degree? How are your goals tied to your desires and expectations?
- **Time-bound.** Set a timeframe for the goals. When you evaluate how far you've come toward achieving your goals, you'll have a better idea of how to assess and set these goals.

Apply these criteria to your work and personal life. If your goals don't meet these criteria, adjust them accordingly so you'll be in a better position to evaluate them next time.

Exercise: Did you uncover any surprises when you assessed your progress toward your goals? What goals did you accomplish? What types of goals were most difficult for you? List any goals you believe you should have been able to check off your list, but you did not finish, and indicate the obstacles that prevented you from doing so. Be honest. Write down steps to take in the future to help ensure you do achieve the goals you set for yourself. For example, you may want to remember to spend 10 minutes each night tackling a particular goal. Or, you'll commit to becoming better organized at work by setting up your morning paperwork before you leave each night. Every step has the potential to improve your chances to achieve your goals.

Goals:

_____

_____

_____

_____

_____

_____

_____

Reason not accomplished:

_____

_____

_____

_____

_____

_____

_____

_____

Action plan:

_____

_____

_____

_____

_____

_____

_____

_____

_____

_____

Identify Ways to Accomplish Missed Goals

Once you understand reasons why you're making progress or not, you should identify what you can do better. Do you need to delegate any tasks (including tasks at home)? Is it appropriate to ask for help (at work or at home)?

Exercise: Seek Help With Your Goals

Make a list of other people you want to involve in helping you accomplish your goals. Who can help you accomplish your plans? Is your boss the best resource? Perhaps you have a mentor who may be able to help you. Review tips about how to ask for help in Chapter 8. Based on your goals and challenges, decide who to turn to for help and what to ask them. Use this worksheet to prepare before you approach anyone for help:

For work goals:

What I need to do:

_____

_____

_____

_____

_____

What type of help I need:

_____

_____

_____

_____

_____

Mistakes made:

_____

_____

_____

_____

_____

Plans to address mistakes:

_____

_____

_____

_____

_____

Suggestions of people who may be able to help:

_____

_____

_____

_____

_____

For personal goals:
What I need to do:

_____

_____

_____

_____

_____

What type of help I need:

_____

_____

_____

_____

_____

Mistakes made:

_____

_____

_____

_____

_____

Plans to address mistakes:

_____
_____
_____
_____
_____

Suggestions of people who may be able to help:

_____
_____
_____
_____
_____

Implement Changes

The benefit of assessing and re-assessing your progress and identifying obstacles in your way is to help you make changes and plan differently the next time. When you are aware of what you need to do differently to accomplish your goals, you can move forward confidently, knowing you will be able to do better next time.

In Summary: Action Tips

When you make yourself accountable for your plans, you'll make a point to review your progress, and assess and make changes.

- Evaluate your work, and if you participate in a company-sanctioned review process, prepare for it.
- Keep records, review your checklists, and prepare for constructive criticism.

- Conduct your own review, and identify any inefficiencies that affect you.
- Review your goals, and seek help if necessary if you are not meeting them.
- Make changes you believe will help propel you in the right direction, and start again on the path to accomplishing what you hope to do.

13 How to Avoid Procrastination

You've heard the quotes about procrastination. "Don't put off until tomorrow what you can do today." Or, perhaps you adhere to the opposite adage, "Never put off until tomorrow what may be done the day after tomorrow just as well." My high school English teacher, Michael Raftery, notes, "Procrastination is the crab grass in the lawn of life." Ultimately, when it comes to planning your time and your life, the most true quote may be, "A year from now you may wish you had started today." Since no one can predict the future, the best approach should be, "Don't wait. The time will never be just right."

If you're waiting for a "perfect" time to take a big step in your life, whether it's for personal or professional reasons, it's unlikely the time will ever come. It's more likely you'll need to just dive into change and embrace the messy aspects that come with trying to achieve new goals while in the midst of a busy, sometimes chaotic life.

Not surprisingly, just as there are many quotes about procrastination, there are many tips and methods to avoid it. Considering the number of distractions most people have in their lives—including social media, 24-hour news, opportunities to binge-watch an entire television series, not to mention the general distractions of everyday life—if you procrastinate, you're in good company. The key is to learn how to avoid and overcome it.

Joseph Ferrari, PhD, is a professor of psychology and author of *Still Procrastinating? The No-Regrets Guide to Getting it Done.* In an interview on the American Psychological Association's website, he explained, "We all put tasks off . . . research has found that 20 percent of U.S. men and women are chronic procrastinators. They delay at home, at work, in school, and in relationships. These 20 percent make procrastination their way of life." While people with clinical depression or phobias may be more likely to procrastinate, those groups don't represent 20 percent of the population. Clearly, it's a major issue that affects many people.

Why Do People Procrastinate?

Frances Booth, author of *The Distraction Trap: How to Focus in a Digital World*, suggested several reasons why people procrastinate in an article for *Forbes*.

You Don't Really Want to Do the Task

For example, if you are procrastinating on applying for a job, perhaps you are ambivalent about making a move or you don't really want a new job, after all. If you've been putting off making a call, maybe you don't actually want to talk to the person you've been avoiding.

It's Too Difficult, Too Easy, or Too Boring

Maybe you need a more challenging (or simple) task that will encourage you to move forward. If this sounds familiar to you, carefully evaluate the items on your to-do list that have been moving from week to week. Are you bored by the items? How can you make it more interesting and fulfilling to accomplish the goal? If the task is too difficult, what will you need to put in place to allow you to accomplish it?

It's Too Overwhelming

This may sound familiar to a lot of people. It's not unusual to procrastinate when the task seems too big or daunting. In this case, the best approach is usually to break down the big task into smaller, more manageable parts. For example, *writing a new resume* sounds like a big job, but *list all your jobs and dates worked* may not be very difficult. Of course, when you break a big task into smaller parts, the result will be a longer list of things to do, but each individual item should be easier to complete than the bigger assignment.

Fatigue and Needing a Break

If it's been a long day and you are still trying to plow through your to-do list, it's easy to look for ways to avoid finishing the work. Perhaps it makes better sense to take a well-timed break.

Fear of Failure or Fear of Success

Do you sometimes procrastinate on big changes because you're not sure what might happen if you pursue them? If this may contribute to your hesitancy, take some time to weigh the pros and cons of moving forward or not. Make an educated choice about whether or not to pursue the plan.

Exercise: Why Do You Procrastinate?

Have you ever stopped to ask yourself why you procrastinate? Maybe now is a good time! Think about the last time you delayed working on a project or handling a deadline. Why did you wait until the last minute, or put off starting to work? Do you believe you work best under stress? Do you really not have time to get things done, so the result is delaying the inevitable? Evaluate your motivations. Write down reasons why you procrastinate. Later in the chapter, another exercise will suggest you identify ways to overcome those reasons.

_____

_____

_____

_____

_____

_____

_____

_____

_____

_____

_____

_____

_____

_____

Risks Procrastinators Take

Do you feel as if you're always working without any breaks? Are you spending so many of your work hours procrastinating and not getting anything done that you never have downtime? This is one risk of spending time checking email or social media, staring out into space, or daydreaming instead of working. It's possible to feel like you've spent the entire day "working," when, in fact, you've procrastinated away all of that time with no end product to show for your efforts.

Constant procrastinators also suffer a lot of stress, according to Ferrari. Worrying about how to get the work done can add a lot of extra pressure, which may wear down the immune system and make procrastinators more likely to get sick. Procrastination can compromise health (because people put off or delay sleep, exercise, or eating well). Procrastinators may put themselves at financial risk by failing to pay bills on time. Other dangerous things to procrastinate about include car or home maintenance, not paying taxes, or failing to renew professional licenses. Relationships also suffer when people procrastinate too much. While a belated birthday card may not end a friendship, if you constantly bring work home because you can't get it done in the office, you may have a difficult time maintaining friendships or family time.

How to Break the Procrastination Cycle

Researchers believe procrastinating is not a simple time management problem, even though time management techniques can be helpful to address the issue. If you are afraid of failure (or success), or simply paralyzed and unable to move forward with your goals, you'll want to reach out for counseling or specific advice to help overcome the bigger issue that may be holding you back from getting ahead. Do not underestimate the ways in which your fears may prevent you from achieving your goals.

If you procrastinate primarily because you need help managing your time, these tips and tricks may help overcome the problem.

Set a Deadline

Give yourself a deadline. Have you seen the quote, "A goal without a deadline is just a dream?" If you don't hold yourself accountable to a timeframe, whether it's a long-term goal or something you need to accomplish right away, it's unlikely you'll ever achieve anything. As noted in Chapter 8, it's best to create a detailed timeline and break up large projects into manageable pieces, each with deadlines.

Jacqui Barrett Poindexter, Chief Career Writer at *Career Trend*, explains how she uses deadlines and a desktop task timer to power through her writing tasks:

> *I work for an hour straight (and only an hour), with a very specific production goal in mind. I whoosh through it to completion, with the caveat that I can edit and clean it up afterward. It's amazing how well we perform and think (and the quality of our work) when we have time/production constraints.*

Break Big Projects Down

Just as your lists include categories and sub-categories, break down your projects and plans into smaller chunks to help avoid feeling overwhelmed and discourage procrastination.

A contact of mine mentioned great advice a realtor gave her about packing up her home to ready it for sale. She had tried to de-clutter it many times, but it was a big job due to the amount of things she accumulated in 15 years. She recounted:

> *I must have looked like I was going to throw up when she told me I needed to de-clutter and pack up all of our personal*

belongings. She told me to pack two boxes per night to make it more manageable. In no time, I finished several closets, plus all but two bookcases. We've thrown out or donated about three-dozen bags and boxes of things. It's brilliant to break it down into an ongoing, manageable project.

Be Accountable

Tell people about your goals, and find an "accountability buddy" who will help encourage you to move forward with your goals. Just as people are more likely to exercise if a trainer or friend is expecting them at the gym, you'll be more likely to follow through if you tell someone your plans and that person can check in with you to ask about your progress. This can be a friend or family member, but many people choose to hire a coach, instead. If you ask your friend or partner to keep you accountable, the check-ins may feel more like nagging and prevent forward progress. If you don't want to hire someone to help and don't want to rely on a friend or family member, search for accountability groups or mastermind programs. These can be online chats or in-person groups of people, all trying to accomplish their individual goals. You don't need to be in the same field as someone else to help them with accountability. All you need to do is understand their timeline and have a general sense of what's required to achieve their goals. Similarly, a mentor may also be able to help you stay accountable, if he or she is willing to step into an active, regular mentoring role.

Social media can help you stay accountable. Instead of turning to Facebook or other online tools to continue to procrastinate and avoid your work, announce a plan online and ask your community to check in with you to track your progress. Dieters sometimes do this successfully. Some people announce their plans to become sober or to quit smoking and request help from their online communities. As long as your plan is public, you may want to say, "I'm planning to finish writing my novel by the end of next month. Please check in with me to help me stay on track, and you'll be the first to read it." Or, "I'm making a long-term plan to earn a certification in meeting planning. It's going to take a lot of advance planning, but my personal deadline is one year from now. Please keep me on track by asking about my progress."

Find and meet people who already accomplished what you want to do. These people can take mentor roles or simply provide a bit of advice to inspire you. It's a good idea to spend time with people who are action oriented and focused. Research shows spending time with strong-willed people can actually improve your self-control. A study in *Psychological Science* says people who have low self-control can improve their discipline by spending time with people who have the desirable traits. Surround yourself with people who inspire you to take action, and you'll be more likely to accomplish your plans.

Eliminate Obstacles

Look around—Is your workspace itself a huge distraction? You're setting yourself up to fail if you don't tailor your environment to help ensure you are as successful as possible. If you can't get work done at home, find somewhere else to work. Go to a coffee shop or find office space elsewhere so you won't be distracted by anything.

If you can't get any work done in your office because there are so many distractions, identify ways to steal some private time. Either work in an office with a closed door (if there is one), or tell people you have a specific deadline you must reach and ask for no interruptions during a certain period of time during the day. If you have to tape a sign to your back asking no one to interrupt you, do it!

Is one of your obstacles overthinking the problem? Try not to overcomplicate the situation. Keep in mind, "The perfect is the enemy of the good." In other words, if you never do anything unless it is perfect, you're unlikely to even accomplish something good. Do not procrastinate because it's not the perfect scenario.

Just as you should try to eliminate the psychological reasons you may be delaying your work, do everything in your power to avoid any physical weaknesses. For example, if you can't help but check your phone every time it buzzes, put the phone elsewhere so you won't be distracted every few minutes.

Susan Pogorzelski, author of *Gold in the Days of Summer* and an International Book Award Finalist, suggests using the Freedom app. She explains:

> *Freedom is my favorite app when I'm writing—*
> *it blocks websites like Facebook and Twitter so*
> *I'm less compelled to hit refresh immediately to review*
> *my social media streams after every sentence I write.*

Take advantage of technology and use an app to cut down on temptation. Disable any sounds or notifications on your computer that may distract you from your work, and consider shutting down programs you can easily check (such as email) so you won't be tempted to use them when you should be productive.

USE TECHNOLOGY TO AVOID DISTRACTIONS

If you like the idea of being "locked out" of distractions, Amy Spencer offered several additional suggestions in *Time* magazine. In addition to Freedom (macfreedom.com), which disables your Internet for an allotted amount of time, RescueTime (rescuetime.com) charts your online time and provides a clear picture of how you are spending (or wasting) your time. LeechBlock (addons.mozilla.org) works with Firefox so you can block certain sites for periods you choose.

Exercise: Choose an App
Review these apps or others your friends recommend. Use one for a week. Do you notice a difference in your productivity?

Perhaps tapping into some of the productivity methods described in Chapter 9 will help keep you moving toward your goal. For example, use the Pomodoro Method or time boxing. Writer and marketing consultant Corey-Jan Albert explains how she gets work done:

> *I follow the 20-minute rule. That is, I commit to work on the project without distraction for 20 minutes. By the time 20 minutes have passed, I'm usually on enough of a roll that I can make significant progress or finish the task.*

Tap Into Your Motivations

What really motivates you and helps you get things done? Is there a reward (beyond simply finishing a big or small task) that might encourage you to finish what's on your list? Do you need to break things down into manageable tasks to even begin to accomplish what's on your list?

Educator and writer Kathy Mathews motivates herself by breaking down tasks and including rewards. She explains:

> *If I write it on a list, I will do it. But if it's something I hate doing, I break it down and include a reward. For example, rather than write, "Pay bills," (which would take a lot of steps and result in one check mark), I expand my list to include all of the smaller steps. For example: "Open all bill envelopes," "Recycle inserts and envelopes," "Organize bills by dates due," "Schedule payments online," and "Enter payments in Quicken." My reward is five check marks on my list and 25 minutes playing on Facebook.*

Whether or not you created a vision board, as recommended in Chapter 8, decide if visualizing yourself accomplishing your goals may inspire you. Close your eyes and picture yourself in a clean office space, or heading up the department at work. Can you psych yourself into being excited about taking the steps needed to accomplish those goals?

Hunter College student Corrina Blau successfully "tricks" herself into avoiding procrastination. She explains:

> *I used to plan my all-nighters about a week in advance. Working at 3 a.m. is great for finishing a long paper, but bad for waking up to go to class the next morning. So, I chose a block of time that was convenient and pretended I had already procrastinated for weeks and felt the stress of having to deliver a finished product in a few hours. Then, I was super productive and finished the project (or most of it) and could enjoy the rest of the time before the actual deadline, feeling like a boss.*

Do you like to win? Incorporate a gaming strategy into your goal setting. If you have an unexciting project, create a game of getting it done. Plan to get a certain amount done in 10 or 20 minutes and see if you can beat the clock. If you get into a groove, you could get a lot done in less time than you might have expected.

You may not need to try to trick yourself into being stressed or play a game to motivate yourself. John Youngblood, a small business owner, entrepreneur, and proud bearded collie owner, explains:

> *I fully embrace procrastination as one of my many delightful personality quirks. That said, when there is something unpleasant that has to be done, I will connect it to something very pleasant. For instance, in order for me to prepare my tasty pasta dinner tonight, I must first do the dishes that I decided to leave in the sink last night. That works for me.*

Another tip to help tap into your personal motivations is to either choose to start with the most or least exciting part of the project first. If you're really dreading one aspect of an assignment and you're procrastinating because you don't want to do something, promise yourself a reward and get the worst part done. Then, you'll be free to move ahead on the rest of the work. On the other hand, if you're really excited about a particular part, but are procrastinating because of the piece you don't want to do, go ahead and finish the fun part and then convince yourself the boring or difficult part isn't so bad, after all, since you'd rather finish it than have it hanging over your head.

Reward Yourself

Reward yourself for big and small accomplishments. You may plan to buy yourself a treat or take that long needed run or walk once you get something checked off your list. If you need to raise the stakes, consider depriving yourself of something you really want to do if you don't meet a certain milestone. For example, if you don't finish a particular task, you won't attend a friend's party. If necessary, plan a series of rewards to motivate you to reach your goals.

Exercise: Determine Methods to Overcome Procrastination
If you completed the exercise to help determine why you procrastinate, it should be easier to help yourself overcome the problem. List which of the techniques in this chapter you plan to incorporate to help you get your work done faster.

_____

_____

_____

_____

_____

_____

_____

_____

_____

_____

_____

_____

_____

_____

_____

_____

Just Do It!

Sometimes, all the games and tricks and rewards aren't enough and you need to buckle down and do the work. On a personal note, I'd like to give some insight into how I wrote this chapter, as it may help inspire procrastinators. This is the last chapter in several books I've written over the past few months, and I've been striving to get to this point for some time. With many obligations, I did not move quickly toward my goal of finishing, and the deadline was coming quickly. Since I normally submit work ahead of schedule, not being close to finished was stressful. However, with a firm deadline, I moved through the last chapters and amusedly remembered the last chapter planned was about procrastination. Recognizing I should take my own advice, I implemented several of the tips to finish this chapter in record time.

First, I turned to my online friends and community for accountability and assistance. I posted on Facebook that I planned to finish this chapter and I gave myself a firm deadline for when I expected to have it done.

I asked for help. The quotes in this chapter come from people connected to me from almost every sphere in my life, including high school teachers, a niece, and friends and colleagues I met more recently. Having their insights to share helped make this chapter the most fun to write, and the words came more quickly.

When I was tempted to delve into other projects or to review email, I reminded myself to avoid distractions, or I wouldn't achieve my stated goal. The double reward of being able to thank everyone and announce I finished the chapter (and the book) hung over me and motivated each new paragraph.

Finally, I relocated myself to my office, worked in uninterrupted quiet, and put aside other obligations in order to finish this one.

I hope these tips and insights, which helped me finish a big project, motivates and inspires you to do the same and to accomplish your big goals.

My colleague, Camille Roberts, CEO of CC Career Services and a federal career consultant, congratulated me on finishing this chapter and commented:

> *When it comes to making changes in your life, you have to want it more than anything. Procrastinating only delays what you deserved all along.*

In Summary: Action Tips

Procrastination will prevent you from accomplishing your life and work goals. That's a great reason to overcome it. Consider incorporating these tips into your plans to help ensure you get your work done and make forward progress on your plans.

- Decide why you procrastinate and recognize the risks of continuing in that cycle.
- Adapt new strategies to help you get your work done.
- Set a deadline.
- Break down big projects into smaller, more manageable pieces.
- Find an accountability partner to keep you on track.
- Avoid obstacles that tend to delay you from your work.
- Use technology, whether as basic as a timer or as sophisticated as an app to track your time.
- Identify your motivations. Should you compete with someone and make getting the work done a game? What rewards would help encourage you to work harder?
- Put the right combination of things in place and just do it!

Conclusion

This entire book is all about putting the right combination of things in place to get ahead at work and in life. On the surface, "just do it" may seem like a cliché. Consider it a reminder—it's up to you to accomplish your goals. When you have goals in mind and a plan in place, no one can stop you from achieving them.

If you thought you were too busy to get anything else productive done in your day, hopefully you're inspired to create a vision board and to be strategic about your short- and long-term goals. Maybe you've already created a punch out list to tackle the items you never seem to check off your list, and identified some time pockets you can fill by marking them off your to-do list. Or, you've tapped into some time saving apps to help you focus and avoid multi-tasking to the point of getting nothing done. Only time will tell how much you can accomplish when you follow even a few of the time-saving suggestions and recommendations included in these chapters.

Use this book to meet your goals head on. Don't drown in the details, make your list, check it twice, and move forward confidently—knowing you're in control of your own destiny!

NOTES

NOTES

NOTES

NOTES